PSYCHOLOGICAL WARFARE

DESTROYING THE POWER OF NEGATIVE WORDS & NEGATIVE THINKING

(SELF-HELP MANUAL)

By: Dr. Charissee Lewis

ISBN: 978-1-934905-07-4

PSYCHOLOGICAL WARFARE:
Destroying the Power of Negative Words & Negative Thinking

Copyright © DR. CHARISSEE LEWIS, 2017

PSYCHOLOGICAL WARFARE:
Destroying the Power of Negative Words & Negative Thinking

It is our prayer and declaration that you would maintain a Spirit of Integrity concerning the knowledge shared with you in this manual. Meaning, when using the information in this book publicly, you would give author proper recognition and acknowledgement for the knowledge, work, experience, research, and labor of development of this book.

No part of this manual may be reproduced by mimeograph process or by another method of duplication unless expressed written permission has been granted by Dr. Charissee Lewis.

Thank you in advance for you countenance of righteousness and obedience.

Ecclesiastes 12:14

For God shall bring every work into judgment, with every secret thing, whether *it be* good, or whether *it be* evil.

ISBN: 978-1-934905-07-4

WORLDWIDE KINGDOM PUBLISHING
1911 Horger St.,
Lincoln Park, Michigan 48146
www.drcharissseelewis.com
Drcharisseelewis@icloud.com

Copyright © DR. CHARISSEE LEWIS, 2017

PSYCHOLOGICAL WARFARE:
Destroying the Power of Negative Words & Negative Thinking

Copyright © DR. CHARISSEE LEWIS, 2017

PSYCHOLOGICAL WARFARE:
Destroying the Power of Negative Words & Negative Thinking

PREFACE

Have you noticed the signs of the times? There is an increase of violence, throughout the universe. Too many people are hopeless and disappointed by demonic assaults and mental challenges? Do you really understand how your spiritual reaction affects your natural environment? Are you aware of what kind of spiritual activity is occurring in your atmosphere? It is quite obvious we are living in evil times; satan and his cohorts have intensified their warfare against the souls of men. For centuries, he has manipulated, magnified, and maneuvered aggressively against humanity to hold us captive through the wickedness of our own minds. He has gone through great extremes to create demonic systems to bring this generation into massive oppression. Through the use of subliminal messages, satan has discovered ways to covertly invade our spirit and soul with evil. He has corrupted our entertainment with a deeper level of perversion, to alter what is good and wholesome. The movies we watch are infiltrated with

Copyright © DR. CHARISSEE LEWIS, 2017

PSYCHOLOGICAL WARFARE:
Destroying the Power of Negative Words & Negative Thinking

scenes of cursing, violence, murder, witchcraft, rebellion, betrayal, and perversion, including homosexuality and lesbianism. Most of the music today, is very explicit and persuasive in its lyrics inciting and inviting young people to engage in corruption and perversion before they become adults. We are definitely living in the last days.

The bible tells us in the last days, we would be exposed to danger and wickedness. This is confirmed by the passage on the below,

II Timothy 3:1-5

This know also, that in the last days perilous times shall come. For men shall be lovers of their own selves, covetous, boasters, proud, blasphemers, disobedient to parents, unthankful, unholy, Without natural affection, trucebreakers, false accusers, incontinent, fierce, despisers of those that are good, Traitors, heady, highminded, lovers of pleasure more than lovers of God; Having a form of godliness, but denying the power thereof: from such turn away.

It is obvious we need the wisdom of God to overcome the negative forces which are challenging to us on a daily basis. We need instruction, guidance, and the power of God to press through negative words and negative thoughts. For too long, we have missed the blessings of the Lord, because

PSYCHOLOGICAL WARFARE:
Destroying the Power of Negative Words & Negative Thinking

of emotional oppression, a negative mindset, and negative words. In this book, we show you how to dismantle and annihilate the stronghold of negativity. We will share with you keys and strategies to expose and destroy the spirit of negativism, spoken by you and those around you. As you accept new knowledge, and impartation from the word of God; you will shift your mindset into a new paradigm and receive the ability to change your thought patterns from the negative to the positive. As a result, you will no longer speak from a negative perception, but you shall speak with great optimism. Through a positive mindset, you will see, enjoy, and experience life changes for the development of healthy a mind, healthy living, and a successful life in the Kingdom of God.

PSYCHOLOGICAL WARFARE:
Destroying the Power of Negative Words & Negative Thinking

PSYCHOLOGICAL WARFARE:
Destroying the Power of Negative Words & Negative Thinking

DEDICATION

This book is dedicated to those who have been bound by negative words and negative thinking. Our prayer is that you will receive new knowledge and truth from the word of God to destroy the spirit of negativity out of your life; and begin to live your life in the spirit of liberty with a positive perspective and the activation of a healthy mind.

This book is also dedicated to those who have been used by satan to speak negatively and demonically against the work of the kingdom of God. My prayer is, this book will show you your errors; and compel you to be healed and delivered from all roots of negativity, in Jesus' Name.

PSYCHOLOGICAL WARFARE:
Destroying the Power of Negative Words & Negative Thinking

SPECIAL THANKS

Special thanks to my son, Pastor Rudy M Lewis, Jr., thank you for all of your love and support, I appreciate your leadership, gifts, and diversities!

Special thanks to my daughter Seer Teaira L. Lewis, I love you for motivating me to complete this book, thank you for inspiring me to complete this assignment!

Special thanks to my Church family LIQUID FIRE TRAINING CENTER, WPKM, and all the APOSTOLIC LEADERS, CHURCHES, and MINISTRIES of WKNC, thank you for allowing me to minister to you and your children. May God continue to bless us corporately as a strong nation with healthy minds to be a positive voice to the Kingdom of God!

PSYCHOLOGICAL WARFARE:
Destroying the Power of Negative Words & Negative Thinking

INTRODUCTION

Do you know what we speak reveals how we think? Do you know the words we speak, influence our atmosphere and environment? The human mind is perplexed and consists of many dimensions that are profound to the existence of humanity. It is amazing how, what we hear and believe can affect our thoughts and behavior. God created us as triune beings; we are a trichotomy: meaning there are three parts which makes up mankind. These three parts consists of spirit, soul, and body. We can be affected spiritually, emotionally, mentally, physically, and psychologically when we hear negativity. Words are very powerful whether they are positive or negative; they have an effect on our total being. Words are alive! Every time we speak, there are cycles of creativity, reactions, and manifestations in the realm of the spirit, which causes our words to be actuated in the natural realm. We should speak what God speaks concerning us. The bible tells us that His words are spirit and life.

PSYCHOLOGICAL WARFARE:
Destroying the Power of Negative Words & Negative Thinking

St. John 6:63

It is the spirit that quickeneth; the flesh profiteth nothing: the words that I speak unto you, they are spirit and they are life.

The way in which we communicate, respond, and answer with our words can determine the quality of success, we may achieve on our road of destiny and in our entire lifetime!

In the last decade, there has been an increase in negativity throughout the universe. The voice of negativity has spread like an epidemic on all levels of existence. Satan has launched a series of attacks against the psyche of man. One major avenue he uses on a daily basis is the radio, internet, and television. The media constantly invade our homes with bad news. News reporters continuously compete with one another to bring us new insights on devastating and traumatic events. There have been numerous amounts of murders throughout the land. There has been an increased accounts of husbands killing their own wives. In time

PSYCHOLOGICAL WARFARE:
Destroying the Power of Negative Words & Negative Thinking

pasts, there has been perpetual reports of the murder and dismemberment of Tara Grant, unfortunately by her own husband. The daily report of this inhumane murder was a tool the devil used, to transfer the same demons into the homes of dysfunctional marriages. Unfortunately, bad events of this sort becomes profitable and sells, through an increase of viewing ratings, and providing a very lucrative business for tabloid magazines. The fact of the matter is, bad news, and negative news sells and bring in lots of money. It is sad to say, it seems people are more eager to hear, speak, and think negatively instead of focusing on the positive, and wonderful news of success.

We are engaged in major psychological warfare, fighting vigorously for the sanity and mental health of humanity. Satan is busy bombarding the minds of man with negative thoughts and words that holds the heart of man captive by darkness. He has intensified the warfare to a level of emotionalism and intellectualism, whereby he challenges the word of God in the heart of the believer by bombarding the mind with negative thoughts.

PSYCHOLOGICAL WARFARE:
Destroying the Power of Negative Words & Negative Thinking

Through the oppression of the mind; negative beliefs overwhelm the heart of the believer and influences him to speak negativity in his atmosphere. As a result, the believer is blinded, ensnared, trapped, and defeated by his own negative words. Words have the ability to create, whether they are positive or negative they influence and shape our atmosphere. The bible tells us death and life is determined by what we speak, according to *Proverbs 18:21*. The bible also instructs us directly about the effects of vain words.

Proverbs 18:21

Death and life is in the power of the tongue: and they that love it shall eat the fruit thereof.

Job 16: 3-4

Shall vain words have an end? or what emboldeneth thee that thou answerest? I also could speak as ye do: if your soul were in my soul's stead, I could heap up words against you, and shake mine head at you.

Proverbs 15:1-2

A soft answer turneth away wrath: but grievous words stir up anger. The tongue of the wise useth knowledge aright: but the mouth of fools poureth out foolishness.

Copyright © DR. CHARISSEE LEWIS, 2017

PSYCHOLOGICAL WARFARE:
Destroying the Power of Negative Words & Negative Thinking

As you have read, negative thoughts and negative words cause death, stagnation and foolishness. Perpetuating the ugliness we see, hear, perceive, and experience through negative conversations can affect our entire well-being.

In conclusion, there is an urgency for us to combat satan with a new fire of truth that can only be imparted from truth, prayer, and the revelation of the word of God. In this self-help manual, we shall uncover the stronghold of negativity. We will give you keys to identify the roots of negativity. We will assist you in destroying negative thoughts and negative word curses that have been spoken over your life. Lastly, we shall share with you scripture to encourage you to change your attitude and disposition. Through the acceptance of the word of God, and inner healing, you will gain new strength to develop a spiritual mind, and a positive view on life. Get ready to enter a supernatural realm of change. The changes you shall receive will give you a new authority to overcome psychological warfare and you shall gain spiritual strength to ***destroy the power of negative words and negative thinking!***

PSYCHOLOGICAL WARFARE:
Destroying the Power of Negative Words & Negative Thinking

Romans 8:5-8

For they that are after the flesh do mind the things of the flesh; but they that are after the Spirit the things of the Spirit.
For to be carnally minded is death; but to be spiritually minded is life and peace.
Because the carnal mind is enmity against God: for it is not subject to
the law of God, neither indeed can be.
So then they that are in the flesh cannot please God.

PSYCHOLOGICAL WARFARE:
Destroying the Power of Negative Words & Negative Thinking

NEGATIVITY IN THE REAR

No more negative sensations,
We are walking in a realm of new revelation.
Seeking truth and finding the real
Devil, no longer can you make mental deals.
Our mind is clear….
From all fear!

No more negative feelings,
We are free from anxiety
And satan's bribery.
We speak what is true,
We see in the new…

No more negative thoughts, do we hear.
No longer do we perceive,
what the devil wants to appear……
God has given us power to
destroy all negativity in the rear!

PSYCHOLOGICAL WARFARE:
Destroying the Power of Negative Words & Negative Thinking

From the Desk of Dr. Charissee Lewis;

To the People of God, I encourage you to remain prayerful while reading this manual. Upon writing this book, I experienced extensive warfare and major interference. I must say through the Grace and Glory of God; I was able to complete this assignment. I realized with a greater understanding the authority we truly have in the words that we speak. I am determined to go deeper in this realm of knowledge and to share with the people of God; the power we have when we say what heaven is saying concerning our situations. The purpose of the manual is to destroy the power of negative words and negative thinking. I am sure many of us have been victimized by the effects of negative speaking. Through the word of God, revelation and experience you will receive an impartation to destroy all negativity out of your life. It is my prayer that the Body of Christ would change our conversation and speak the Word of the Lord wherever we go! For we are an extension of heaven …here on earth! May God continue to bless you, richly!

In His Presence,
Dr. C. Lewis

PSYCHOLOGICAL WARFARE:
Destroying the Power of Negative Words & Negative Thinking

TABLE OF CONTENTS

Call of Integrity
Preface
Dedication
Special Thanks
Introduction

UNCOVERING NEGATIVITY   p. 21

1) Understanding Psychological Warfare   p. 23
2) Identifying Roots of Negativity   p. 38
3) The Stronghold of Negativism   p. 62
4) The Power of the Tongue: Word Curses   p. 80

DESTROYING NEGATIVITY   p.107

5) Mind Battles: Destroying Negative Thinking   p.109
6) Exposing Wicked Imaginations   p.129
7) Identifying Emotional Abuse   p.165
8) The Spirit of Witchcraft   p.179

DEVELOPING A POSITIVE MIND   p.185

9) Adjusting Your Attitude   p.187
10) Understanding the Value of Your Thoughts   p.198
11) Developing a Healthy Spiritual Mind   p.201
12) The Beautiful Healthy Mind   p.228

PSYCHOLOGICAL WARFARE:
Destroying the Power of Negative Words & Negative Thinking

PSYCHOLOGICAL WARFARE:
Destroying the Power of Negative Words & Negative Thinking

UNCOVERING NEGATIVITY

PSYCHOLOGICAL WARFARE:
Destroying the Power of Negative Words & Negative Thinking

PSYCHOLOGICAL WARFARE:
Destroying the Power of Negative Words & Negative Thinking

Chapter One

UNDERSTANDING PSYCHOLOGICAL WARFARE

Are you aware of the phenomenal increase of mental challenges plaguing people of today? The rise of mental health problems has reached its peak in today's generation. People of all nations are being harassed by attacks on their minds. It is not uncommon to see a person walking down the street talking to himself, because he hears voices. Mind binding and mind blinding spirits make it difficult for people to make simple decisions. These vile mental spirits purpose is to bind and block the spiritual vision, natural vision, and comprehension of an individual: so he cannot see, hear, understand, and receive truth. The spirit of leviathan is a mind binding and mind blocking spirit. It hinders teachers from teaching students how to learn and increase their reading skills. This ancient spirit negatively affects the mind, and the learning ability of students. As a result, it makes the children's comprehension very low.

PSYCHOLOGICAL WARFARE:
Destroying the Power of Negative Words & Negative Thinking

These are some examples of **psychological warfare**.

Psychological warfare is mental combat. It deals with the opposition of the mind and the will of man. It entails satanic spirits warring against the mental ability of one's mind; thereby causing one to experience spiritual attacks in their mind. It deals with the cognitive function of man by confusing desires, thoughts, words, and inclinations. These inclinations deal with a particular disposition of the mind and character of man. The aim of satan and his co-horts in this kind of warfare, is to cause one to bend or deviate from their true purpose in life. These demonic spirits come to invade the mind with debasing thoughts. In this level of warfare, the enemy uses the spirit of confusion, delusions, and distractions to detour believers from functioning and operating in their Kingdom mandate. Satan's ambition is to cause the believer to abort their Kingdom mission, calling, and destiny. As you can see psychological warfare entails more than mental aberration. It is a deeper spiritual warfare that affects the psyche of man. Its mission is to prevent man from successfully completing any

PSYCHOLOGICAL WARFARE:
Destroying the Power of Negative Words & Negative Thinking

assignment that is associated with the Kingdom of God.

In conclusion, we have prepared an assignment to help you recognize that you are in strategic psychological warfare. Through the method of recognition and the spirit of truth, we hope you will feel secure in engaging in these self-help activities. The self-help activities have been developed to assist you in your process of inner healing and deliverance. It is our prayer that you will partake in all the spiritual activities; we designed at the end of each chapter. Every activity is vital to the sanctification of your spirit and soul. As you complete every assignment there is no doubt, you will be cleansed from negative words and negative thinking. As you continue to read, you will gain new knowledge on how to be victorious in psychological warfare.

* On the next page, we have written some signs, indications, and manifestations of psychological warfare, please check what applies to you.

PSYCHOLOGICAL WARFARE:
Destroying the Power of Negative Words & Negative Thinking

Signs, Indications, and Manifestations of Psychological Warfare

- __Addictions
- __Addiction to Adrenaline
- __Addiction to Pain
- __Addiction to Stress
- __Affliction
- __Aggravation
- __Agitation
- __Angry Behavior
- __Angry Countenance
- __Angry Outburst
- __Angry Thoughts
- __Angry Words
- __Aggressive Anger
- __Anger
- __Anguish
- __Anxiety
- __Anxiety Disorders
- __Back Biting
- __Back Spasms
- __Bad attitude
- __Betrayal
- __Bitterness
- __Bi-Polar Spirits
- __Black Hearted
- __Blocking spirits
- __Borderline Disorders
- __Bullying

- __Bursting of Emotions
- __Chronic Pain Depression
- __Compromise Deterrence
- __Confusion Deviation
- __Control Dissatisfaction
- __Control Others
- __Controlling Powers
- __Critical
- __Critical Perception
- __Criticize Others
- __Cruelty
- __Cynical
- __Damaged Emotions
- __Deadly Emotions
- __Deception
- __Delusions
- __Dementia
- __Demonic Thoughts
- __Denial
- __Depression
- __Dirty Jokes
- __Dirty Thoughts
- __Distractions
- __Distrust
- __Distrustful Thoughts
- __Doubled Tongued
- __Doubt

Copyright © DR. CHARISSEE LEWIS, 2017

PSYCHOLOGICAL WARFARE:
Destroying the Power of Negative Words & Negative Thinking

Signs, Indications, and Manifestations of Psychological Warfare (Con't)

__Doubtful Thoughts
__Driven to Evil
__Driven to Revenge
__Driven to Rush
__Emotional Attacks.
__Emotional Deficiency
__Emotional Drama
__Emotional Hurts
__Emotional Manipulation
__Emotional Trapped.
__Emotional Trauma
__Emotional Turmoil
__Evil Desires
__Evil Thoughts
__Exaggerate
__Falsely Accusing Others
__False Burdens
__False Mental Perception
__False Obligations
__Familiar Sprits
__Fantasy Lusts
__Fear of Authority
__Fear of Being Left Behind
__Fear of Failure
__Fear of Love

__Fear of Rejection
__Feeling Harassed
__Forgetfulness
__Frustrations
__Gluttony
__Grief
__Guilt
__Hallucinations
__Hatred
__Hearing Voices
__Heartache
__Hidden Motives
__Hostility
__Hurt
__Hypertension
__Illiteracy
__Illusions
__Images of Jealousy
__Images of Tragedy
__Images of War
__Inadequacies
__Indifference
__Indecisions/Indecisiveness
__Indignation
__Inhibitions

Copyright © DR. CHARISSEE LEWIS, 2017

PSYCHOLOGICAL WARFARE:
Destroying the Power of Negative Words & Negative Thinking

Signs, Indications, and Manifestations of Psychological Warfare (Con't)

- __Insanity
- __Insecurities
- __Intellectualism
- __Intense Anger
- __Intimidation
- __Jealous Ambitions
- __Jealous Desires
- __Jealous Rage
- __Jealous Thoughts
- __Jealousy
- __Justify Bad Behavior
- __Liar
- __Lingering Pain
- __Low Comprehension Skills
- __Low Self-Concept
- __Low Self-Esteem
- __Low Spirits
- __Magnification
- __Manic Depression
- __Manipulation
- __Mental Anguish
- __Mental Attacks
- __Mental Blockages
- __Mental Challenges
- __Mental Confusion
- __Mental Deficiency
- __Mental Illness
- __Mental Oppression
- __Mental Stress
- __Mental Struggles
- __Migrane Headaches
- __Mind Battles
- __Mind Blocking Spirits
- __Mind Blurriness
- __Mind Disorders
- __Mood Disorders
- __Negative Attitude
- __Negative Behavior
- __Negative Communications
- __Negative Cycles
- __Negative Disposition
- __Negative Emotions
- __Negative Experiences
- __Negative Inner Vows
- __Negative Memories
- __Negative Patterns
- __Negative Perceptions
- __Negative Responses
- __Negative Thinking
- __Negative Thought Patterns

Copyright © DR. CHARISSEE LEWIS, 2017

PSYCHOLOGICAL WARFARE:
Destroying the Power of Negative Words & Negative Thinking

Signs, Indications, and Manifestations of Psychological Warfare
(Con't)

__Negative Responses
__Occult Spirits
__Offenses
__Oughts
__Overwhelming Emotions
__Panic Attacks
__Pain in Back
__Paranoia
__Phobias
__Physical Pain
__People Pleaser
__Perfectionism
__Pessimistic
__Plotting Evil
__Pretension
__Pride
__Procrastination
__Psychological Games
__Psychotic Disorders
__Racing Thoughts
__Rage
__Repressed Anger
__Rejection
__Resentment
__Retaliation
__Revenge

__Sabatoge
__Schizophrenic
__Secrecy
__Self-Hatred
__Self-Pity Rejection
__Self-Rejection kepticism
__Skepticism orcery
__Sorcery pite
__Spirit of Depression
__Spirit of Leviathan
__Spirit of Octopus
__Spiritual Pain
__Spite
__Spiritual Pain
__Stressful Emotions
__Suppressed Emotions
__Talebearer
__Tension
__Thoughts of Anger
__Thoughts of Confusion Fear
__Thoughts of Fear
__Thoughts of Indecisiveness
__Thoughts of Malice
__Thoughts of Manipulation
__Thoughts of Murder
__Thoughts of Procrastination

Copyright © DR. CHARISSEE LEWIS, 2017

PSYCHOLOGICAL WARFARE:
Destroying the Power of Negative Words & Negative Thinking

Signs, Indications, and Manifestations of Psychological Warfare
(Con't)

__Thoughts of Revenge
__Thoughts of Stubbornness
__Thoughts of Suicide
__Tormenting Spirits
__Toxic Mentality
__Transference of Spirits
__Unbelief
__Uncertainty
__Underlying Emotional Components
__Unforgiveness
__Ungodly Affections
__Ungodly Attitude
__Ungodly Appetitie
__Ungodly Desires
__Ungodly Soul Ties
__Ungodly Thoughts
__Unstable
__Unsure
__Vengeance
__Venomous Words
__Violence
__Visions of Destruction
__Visions of Fear
__Whoredom
__Witchcraft
__Wizardry

PSYCHOLOGICAL WARFARE:
Destroying the Power of Negative Words & Negative Thinking

As you can see there are many signs, symptoms, and manifestations of psychological warfare. As stated earlier, psychological warfare is combat in the mind. It brings the mind into a state of mental oppression and creates negative emotions. The manifestations shared with you are common attitudes, behaviors, dispositions, mindsets, and demonic spirits that may attack and oppress an individual in every area of his life. We exposed the various tricks, and traps the enemy uses to capture the mind of a believer to put him into a state of bondage. The enemy is a master of deception, and he incites events of negativity to perpetuate psychological warfare. It is crucial that you have knowledge of the different manifestations, the enemy may use against you in this area of psychological warfare. We trust you read thoroughly the multiple signs, symptoms, and manifestations of psychological warfare. Now that you have read, recognized, identified, and chosen the demons that are attacking you in psychological warfare; you are ready to begin your process of deliverance. On the following pages, we provided a prayer to engage and

PSYCHOLOGICAL WARFARE:
Destroying the Power of Negative Words & Negative Thinking

activate you to become victorious in the battle of psychological warfare. In the process of maintaining deliverance of the mind, we will reveal to you scriptures and new coping skills to assist you and strengthen you in supporting your mental deliverance. No longer can you allow negative thoughts to bombard your mind. You cannot continue to exist in oppression, depression, suppression, and repression. You are dishonoring yourself and your well-being when trying to navigate through life; without confronting and removing the negative influences, negative feelings, and negative behaviors that are associated with negative thoughts. With the power of God, you will engage and conquer negative thinking. We will show you in this manual you have the power to dismantle, dethrone, and destroy the stronghold of negativity and regain control of your thoughts, words, and actions through the power of the Holy Ghost, prayer, and the word of God. We can do all things through our Lord & Savior Jesus Christ!

PSYCHOLOGICAL WARFARE:
Destroying the Power of Negative Words & Negative Thinking

ENGAGING IN PSYCHOLOGICAL WARFARE

Father in the Name of Jesus Christ, I ask You to forgive me of all my sins, sins of omission, sins of commission; and any thoughts or deeds that are contrary to Your word. Lord, today I repent of the spirit of pride, the armor of satan, and all the demonic spirits that are connected, associated, and affiliated with this stubborn stronghold, in Jesus' Name. Today, I yield to the power of the Holy Spirit and confess my arrogance and self-importance; I choose to come out of denial, in Jesus Name. No longer will I walk in fear and the spirit of offense, tolerating evil spirits in my life, in Jesus' Name. I rebuke and pull down this stronghold that has blinded me from seeing myself the way God sees me, in Jesus' Name. I refute and disallow the spirit of rebellion from influencing my behavior; this demon is linked with the spirit of pride, and has kept me in bondage for too long, in Jesus' Name. The weapons of my warfare are not carnal,

PSYCHOLOGICAL WARFARE:
Destroying the Power of Negative Words & Negative Thinking

ENGAGING IN PSYCHOLOGICAL WARFARE
(con't)

but mighty through God to the pulling down of strongholds casting down imagination and every high thing that exalt itself against the knowledge of God and bringing into captivity every thought to the obedience of Christ; and having in a readiness to revenge all disobedience, when your obedience is fulfilled, according to **II Corinthians 10:4-6**. I break, refute and cast out every demon connected with the psychological warfare I am now battling in my mind; (name and write down every spirit you checked on the previous page _____ I cancel and crush every contract set up by the enemy to torment and control my mind, in Jesus' Name. No weapon that is formed against me shall prosper; and every tongue that shall rise against thee in judgment thou shalt condemn. This is the heritage of the servants of the LORD, and their righteousness is of me, saith the LORD, according

PSYCHOLOGICAL WARFARE:
Destroying the Power of Negative Words & Negative Thinking

ENGAGING IN PSYCHOLOGICAL WARFARE
(con't)

to **Isaiah 54:17**. I loose, and receive the spirit of peace in my mind. I loose positive thoughts and positive emotions, in Jesus' Name. I thank You for a sound and healthy mind, in Jesus' Name. For God hath not given me the spirit of fear; but of power, and of love, and of a sound mind, according to **II Timothy 1:7**, in Jesus' Name. I thank You Lord, for the fruits of the spirit; love, joy, peace, longsuffering, gentleness, goodness, faith, meekness, and temperance: against such there is no law, **Galatians 5:22-23,** in Jesus' Name. No longer will I be oppressed, harassed, pushed, and driven by the enemy, and the pressure of stress in my mind, in Jesus' Name. Today, I accept and believe I am healed, every time the enemy rises up in my mind, I shall refute his lies through the word of God. Thank You, Father God for a new healthy mindset, in the Name of Jesus Christ!

PSYCHOLOGICAL WARFARE:
Destroying the Power of Negative Words & Negative Thinking

In summary, you have just completed the initial engagement of the battle, recognition and identification. Through gaining new understanding of psychological warfare, you were able to specifically see the nature of the conflict. Your honesty in confronting the demons that are operating in your atmosphere is vital to determining the depth of cleansing that shall take place in your inner healing and deliverance process. This is a valuable chapter in laying foundation for deep inner soul cleansing. The enemy operates covertly in our lives, because he does not want us to detect his ability to deceive us on our road of destiny. Know this, he is a master at deception. While reading and activating in the written spiritual assignments of this manual; there is a deliverance mantle and healing impartation being released into you. Reader, it is our prayer that you will complete every assignment honestly, so you can receive the deep inner soul healing and deliverance that you so desperately need. The Holy Spirit is healing your mind, will, emotions, imagination, memory, and

Copyright © DR. CHARISSEE LEWIS, 2017

intellect, even now, saith the Lord of Hosts! Receive it, in the Mighty Name of Our Lord and Savior Jesus Christ!

If you feel you have not been totally honest, dismiss pride and revisit the list at this time, and repeat the prayer. It is not uncommon for us to go back through the list, sometimes demonic spirits remain dormant in the corridors of our minds and they must be invoked to be evicted out of our mind. Deliverance means to be set free from the old paradigms which keep us bound to demonic thought patterns. Reader, do not make excuses for negativity in your life, we encourage right now to get free!

PSYCHOLOGICAL WARFARE:
Destroying the Power of Negative Words & Negative Thinking

Chapter Two

IDENTIFYING ROOTS OF NEGATIVITY

How do you perceive life? Do you see life through a positive view or a negative view? Are you mostly happy or angry? Do you consider yourself a winner or a loser? These are some valuable questions we want you to consider while reading this chapter. Your response will assist you in discovering what kind of thought patterns that are flowing through your mind on a daily basis. A **thought pattern** is a habit of thinking in a certain way, which entails using particular assumptions which can be positive or negative. It is important for us to have positive thought patterns, and not negative thought patterns; because our thoughts influence and impact our daily living which includes our emotions, attitudes, and behaviors. The bible tells us, for as a man thinketh in his heart, *so is* he, according to **Proverbs 23:7**. In other words, whatever a man thinks in his heart, it will be revealed and manifested through his actions. In this

PSYCHOLOGICAL WARFARE:
Destroying the Power of Negative Words & Negative Thinking

chapter, we will expose various negative thought patterns and assist you in a process of deliverance from these negative thoughts. An essential aspect of deliverance is recognition and identification. We have to determine the psychological position of an individual and discover the origin and identity of attitudes and behaviors before we can supply you with a solution. We will share knowledge with you to assist you in discovering, and identifying roots of negativity.

The word **"negative"** lacks positive qualities. It is defined by <u>Webster Dictionary,</u> as being marked by features of hostility, withdrawal, or pessimism that hinders or oppose constructive treatment or development. It means to deny truth, reality, or validity. This word gives the connotation of moving in a direction opposite to a chosen or regular direction and position. It opposes the laws of God. It has an anti position which goes against the norm of conformity. A person who is negative will find it difficult to receive the promises of God; because negativity positions a

PSYCHOLOGICAL WARFARE:
Destroying the Power of Negative Words & Negative Thinking

person's mind in opposition to the mind of Christ. The negative mindset is based in a carnal mindset. It despises that which is good. It rejects truth and embraces the fleshly and the satanic. Let's examine the scriptures in the book of Romans which confirms this fact.

Romans 8:5-8

For they that are after the flesh do mind the things of the flesh; but they that are after the Spirit the things of the Spirit.
For to be carnally minded is death; but to be spiritually minded is life and peace.
Because the carnal mind is enmity against God: for it is not subject to the law of God, neither indeed can be.
So then they that are in the flesh cannot please God.

The scripture above tells us to be carnally minded is death, but to be spiritually minded is life and peace. The carnal mind causes a person to think and desire the sins of the flesh; this kind of mind open portals to the kingdom of darkness. We all know the sins of the flesh opposes the spiritual realm and the laws of God. The scriptures in Galatians confirms this fact let's examine them introspectively.

PSYCHOLOGICAL WARFARE:
Destroying the Power of Negative Words & Negative Thinking

Galatians 5:16-18

This I say then, Walk in the Spirit, and ye shall not fulfill the lust of the flesh.
For the flesh lusteth against the Spirit, and the Spirit against the flesh: and these are contrary the one to the other: so that ye cannot do the things that ye would.
But if ye be led of Spirit, ye are not under the law.

An intricate part of walking in the Spirit is to have a spiritual mind. A **spiritual mind** is a mind with thought patterns that are receptive and submissive to instruction, revelation, illumination, and the knowledge of God. It is a mind that is God-conscious and obedient to the laws of God. The scriptures in the book of Romans and Galatians exposes the state of opposition between the spirit and flesh. As we stated earlier, that the carnal mind do mind the activities of the flesh, and when we fulfill the lust of the flesh; we are operating in a carnal state of thinking, which is negative. The carnal mind is an enemy against God. It is not subject to the laws of God; and it causes a believer to be lawless, disobedient, and rebellious against the principles of God. A carnal minded man

PSYCHOLOGICAL WARFARE:
Destroying the Power of Negative Words & Negative Thinking

cannot please, receive, or obey the laws of God. Negative thought patterns can infiltrate the carnal mind, causing a person to walk in the flesh and manifest negative behavior. A carnal mind with negative thoughts keeps the believer bound by fleshly sins. This is why it is essential for believers to be renewed in the spirit of our minds; and transform from a carnal state of thinking to a spiritual state of thinking. We must understand and develop a spiritual mind to experience life and peace in the Kingdom of God.

In order to be successful in the identification process of our thought patterns, we find it necessary to challenge you to go to the **"root"** of the issue. A root is the beginning of a seed growing inwardly, covertly. It is hidden from our natural view and sometimes our natural understanding. It cannot be seen in the natural realm with our natural vision. It is something that grows underground; it is an organ of absorption, according to <u>Webster's Dictionary</u>. In this segment, we are admonishing you to deal with the root,

PSYCHOLOGICAL WARFARE:
Destroying the Power of Negative Words & Negative Thinking

essential core of your problems. To begin with, when you examine yourself introspectively, you must identify all negative encounters in your life. This process entails identification of negative thought patterns and a reflection of all past experiences. On the next page, we share with you the different kinds of negative thought patterns which are common amongst people who have negative mindsets. In being honest with yourself, you may recognize some characteristics of negativity in your feelings and behavior, which reflect the different kinds of negative thought patterns.

In conclusion, are you ready for a paradigm shift in your mind? The paradigm shift is changing the guidelines, rules, and regulations in which you choose to live. Are you ready to change your thought patterns? If you are ready; then get prepared for a mind transformation by going through the mind renewal process of identifying all negative thought patterns, deliverance from roots of negativity, and healing from all negative experiences!

PSYCHOLOGICAL WARFARE:
Destroying the Power of Negative Words & Negative Thinking

Identifying Negative Thought Patterns

1. A Mindset of Extremities without Balance (All or Nothing Thinking)
- This mentality sees everything in black and white categories, and there are no gray areas or discipline.
- It is a mindset that is rigid and deals with the spirit of perfectionism, selfishness, competition.
- When a person with this mentality is unable to perform or produce; he or she feels like a failure.

2. A Mindset of Catastrophism
- This mentality causes a person to envision an event with a disastrous end.
- This mindset always sees the final result as a catastrophe.
- The person with this mindset will have visions of situations and events ending with tragedy, because this person thoughts gives him or her an outlook of sudden calamity, disaster, and misfortune.

3. A Mindset of Disqualifying the Positive
- This mentality refuses to accept positive experiences by dismissing the joy, and happiness that comes from the experience of a positive situation.

PSYCHOLOGICAL WARFARE:
Destroying the Power of Negative Words & Negative Thinking

Identifying Negative Thought Patterns (con't)

- This is a mindset which devalues the worth of positive experiences, so the person with this thought pattern will continue to see negatively.
- When a person operates in this mentality, his or her thoughts continue to nullify positive experiences; as a result, the person maintains a negative belief that contradicts all positive experiences.

4. A Mindset of Disqualifying the Present
- This mentality causes a person to disregard the joy, and happiness of a present situation, to make him or her feel that what an individual is experiencing now is not good enough.
- This mindset will not allow a person to accept the good in a present situation, so he or she remains in an unhappy negative state.
- This mindset causes a person to miss the positive actions in a present event or situation by deceiving an individual to believe the positive event or situation did not happen.

PSYCHOLOGICAL WARFARE:
Destroying the Power of Negative Words & Negative Thinking

Identifying Negative Thought Patterns (con't)

5. A Mindset of Dwelling on Pain
- This mentality causes a person to focus on painful situations, deceiving one to believe he or she will feel better when dwelling on pain.
- This mindset causes a person to believe he or she feel better when one thinks about or talks about the painful events to others.
- This mindset constantly complains about pain, and do not realize that dwelling on pain will actually magnify pain in one's body.

6. A Mindset of Emotional Reasoning and Rationalization
- This mentality take a position that what one feels or assumes reveals the truth of a situation, and it may not be true.
- A person with this mindset operates in their feelings and the assumption that whatever he or she feels is right and true. This person thinks their negative emotions and feelings reveal and reflect the actual reality of a situation.
- This mindset causes a person to be so emotional he or she maintains a negative belief, because of what he or she may feel.

PSYCHOLOGICAL WARFARE:
Destroying the Power of Negative Words & Negative Thinking

Identifying Negative Thought Patterns (con't)

7. A Mindset of Excessive Need for Approval
- This mentality causes a person to believe he or she must receive the approval and applause of other people in order to be happy.
- This mindset will cause a person to compromise morality, and truth in order to receive favor and acceptance from others.
- This mindset will cause a person to believe if he or she does not win the approval of others; he or she is deceived into thinking one cannot be happy and the other person is angry with him or her.

8. A Mindset of Being Quick to Jump to Conclusions
- This mentality causes a person to make negative assumptions and negative interpretations without any definite facts to support your negative conclusions.
- This mindset causes a person to think someone is reacting or responding to him or her in a negative matter, without investigating truth.
- This mindset also causes a person to be quick to anticipate and conclude that the final results of situations are bad and negative; and he or she feels their prediction is an established fact.

PSYCHOLOGICAL WARFARE:
Destroying the Power of Negative Words & Negative Thinking

Identifying Negative Thought Patterns (con't)

9. A Mindset of Labeling and Mislabeling
- This mentality causes a person to extremely exaggerate and over generalize a situation to make it negative.
- This mindset causes a person to add negative labels to a person or situation.
- This mindset also causes a person to mislabel a situation by describing it with language that incites negative imaginations and emotional attitudes.

10. A Mindset of Negative Mental Filters
- This mentality causes a person to take negative situations and meditate on them until his or her visions of reality become distorted.
- This mindset causes a person to dwell on the negative until their view becomes darken by false impressions and wrong thoughts causing a person to filter out all the good qualities
so he or she focuses on the negative.
- This mindset is infiltrated with negative thoughts because of constantly dwelling on negative defeats; with this mindset everything becomes negative.

PSYCHOLOGICAL WARFARE:
Destroying the Power of Negative Words & Negative Thinking

Identifying Negative Thought Patterns (con't)

11. **A Mindset of Magnification**
    - This mentality causes a person to take important facts of a situation and exaggerate a person's success or failures by using words to magnify important facts.
    - This mindset takes a situation and makes something appear greater than what it really is; only to deceive the view of the true facts. It attacks the imagery of what a person see.
    - This mindset specializes in increasing the perception of a person or situation to distort the authenticity.

12. **A Mindset of Mind Reading**
    - This mentality causes a person to conclude what another person is thinking and he or she has no evidence to prove his or her thoughts about the other person.
    - This mindset causes a person to feel he or she knows what someone is thinking; while passing it to others without confirming if what he or she is feeling is true or false.
    - This mindset causes a person to believe he or she knows the thoughts of others, and that individual influences others to believe the same thoughts without factual evidence.

PSYCHOLOGICAL WARFARE:
Destroying the Power of Negative Words & Negative Thinking

Identifying Negative Thought Patterns (con't)

13. **A Mindset of Minimization**
    - This mentality causes a person to take important facts of a situation and devalue a person's success or failures by using words to decrease essential facts of a particular person or situation.
    - This mindset takes a situation and makes something appear to be the least possible amount in value, or importance.
    - This mindset specializes in minimizing, belittling, and decreasing the perception of a person or situation to distort the authenticity of the person or situation.

14. **A Mindset of Overgeneralization**
    - This mentality causes a person to perceive a negative event or negative action as a perpetual pattern of defeat.
    - This mindset uses words that are excessive to emphasis the common character rather than revealing the specific details about a person or event.
    - This mindset views any single negative event or activity as an external pattern of negativity for everything in life.

PSYCHOLOGICAL WARFARE:
Destroying the Power of Negative Words & Negative Thinking

Identifying Negative Thought Patterns (con't)

15. **A Mindset of Pessimism**
    - This mentality causes a person to believe the evil in the world outweighs the good in the world.
    - This mindset causes a person to expect misfortune, tragedy, or disaster in all circumstances and events.
    - A person with this mindset practice looking at the dark side of a situation, so his or her outlook is always negative.

16. **A Mindset of Personalization**
    - This mentality takes everything so personal that one becomes easily offended by any perception of criticism.
    - This mindset makes a person turn every event as negative onslaught against him or her.
    - This mindset causes a person to be defensive and lash out if he or she slightly feels a negative comment is about him or her.

17. **A Mindset of Should Statements**
    - This mentality refuses to accept the world's reality and causes a person to shape the world to his or her vision of reality.
    - This mindset is usually full of statements of regrets by using words such as: *"should have, would have, or*

PSYCHOLOGICAL WARFARE:
Destroying the Power of Negative Words & Negative Thinking

Identifying Negative Thought Patterns (con't)

could have but whatever the person wanted did not happen….."
- This mindset tries to control relationships based on what a person believes another person should do.

CONSEQUENCES OF NEGATIVE THINKING

As you can see, the consequences of negative thinking hinder us from changing who we are; it is an obstacle and it creates opposition for a person's ability to engage in self-change. It causes a person who is already distorted in his or her pattern of thoughts, to feel intimidated and challenged to make any kind of positive changes concerning self-image. Negative thinking always affects the way a person may see and interact with other people by causing them to perceive a situation in a deceptive view. It has a destructive impact on perception, emotions, and behaviors; because negative thinking instantly hinders us from receiving and achieving what we want. The aim of negative thinking is to bombard our mind with

PSYCHOLOGICAL WARFARE:
Destroying the Power of Negative Words & Negative Thinking

feelings that are not positive. Negative thought patterns, also makes it difficult for a person to accept the promises of God, because of the distortion and demonic oppression that correlates with negative thinking. Many people who think negatively are victimized by anxiety, hurt, pain, isolation, loneliness, depression, suicide, and other negative destructive emotions. These negative emotions dominate and overshadow a person's ability to give love and to receive love. Negative emotions rob a person of their ability to enjoy happy moments and positive events in their lives. It is imperative that believers investigate and identify their process of thinking to determine, if they may be a victim of negative thought patterns. So many people think they are right in their perceptions and thought patterns, but when negativity is a constant voice that whispers in your mind; this is a sure indication that distorted thinking is operating in the function of your mind.

Unfortunately the thought patterns we discussed previously; impact and interfere with the spiritual and

PSYCHOLOGICAL WARFARE:
Destroying the Power of Negative Words & Negative Thinking

natural growth of the believer. The distortion of negative thoughts keeps the mind of believers in a state of spiritual immaturity. When a believer is spiritually immature, it is difficult for him to understand and operate in the spiritual realm and in the mind of faith. His spiritual man is weakened and becomes spiritually unstable by the infiltration of distorted thoughts. These distorted thoughts invade his true identity (spiritual man), perception, and contaminate a person's ability to accept the positive in any situation or event. In order to grow spiritually, we must have a healthy spiritual mind not a negative mind.

Negative thinking also has a negative effect on our perceptions, emotions and behaviors. It alters the way we see others, the way we feel about others, and the way we may behave towards others. Negative thinking has a pattern of damaging our emotions. When people are constantly overwhelmed by negative thoughts and negative words, they do not feel good or happy about themselves and the people that are

PSYCHOLOGICAL WARFARE:
Destroying the Power of Negative Words & Negative Thinking

around them.

Negative thought patterns can ultimately have a detrimental effect on the physical body. The body can become vulnerable to physical attacks, when the mind is weaken by negative opposing thoughts. Negative thoughts open the door to the spirit of worry, anxiety, fear, and stress. These spirits come to stagnate and paralyze the natural body, to stop a person from moving forward in life. Mental health is very crucial to the strength of the physical body. Having a healthy mindset can determine a person's ability to make right or wrong decisions, and succeed or fail in life circumstances.

In conclusion the last 12 pages, we shared the various kinds of Negative Thought Patterns, if necessary reread these pages so you can honestly identify what applies to you. After doing so, we want you to identify negative roots. In the next step, we have a series of exercises to get you acquainted with the inner workings of the Holy Spirit to assist you

PSYCHOLOGICAL WARFARE:
Destroying the Power of Negative Words & Negative Thinking

with identifying the negative roots on the inside of you. Our purpose is to see you set free from the negative roots lying dormant within your mind which influences your daily thinking. It is imperative for us to recognize, identify, and acknowledge root problems. The only way we can be truly set free from negative thought patterns, we must identify situations which open spiritual doors that alter our patterns of thoughts. Sometimes this occurs during childhood experiences or traumatic situations in our lives as adults. Regardless of how it occurred, it is time to be healed!

Reader, on the next few pages we have provided some exercises to walk you through deep inner soul healing. Please take your time and be honest with yourself and allow the Holy Spirit to bring up what is lying dormant in your sub-conscious, so you can be totally cleansed and healed from the roots of negativity that has been influencing your decisions and infiltrating your process of pure decision making.

PSYCHOLOGICAL WARFARE:
Destroying the Power of Negative Words & Negative Thinking

Part I.

- Ask the Holy Spirit to illuminate your heart with His presence and to reveal all hidden areas of hurt and reveal all negative experiences that requires your need for a healing and deliverance.

- Write down all negative experiences in your life that has made a major impact on how you view life, and how you interact with others.

- Write down all negative experiences that has affected your self-esteem, and your perception of your self.

- Write down all traumatic experiences that happen to you from your childhood to this present day.

- Write down the names of those who have violated, disappointed, betrayed, or hurt you in any form in the second portion of **"Roots of Negativity"**.

- Write down names of family members, friends, and people who you love; but they hurt you and you never say anything to them about it.

- Please move forward by following the instructions.

PSYCHOLOGICAL WARFARE:
Destroying the Power of Negative Words & Negative Thinking

Roots of Negativity

1. _____

2. _____

3. _____

4. _____

5. _____

6. _____

7. _____

8. _____

PSYCHOLOGICAL WARFARE:
Destroying the Power of Negative Words & Negative Thinking

Part II.

- With each negative experience, go back and write down the names of those who were involved.

- Write down the names of those who brought you drama, trauma, and pain into your life.

- Write down the names of those you have an ought with, and you have not forgiven.

_____   _____   _____
_____   _____   _____
_____   _____   _____
_____   _____   _____
_____   _____   _____
_____   _____   _____
_____   _____   _____
_____   _____   _____
_____   _____   _____
_____   _____   _____
_____   _____   _____
_____   _____   _____
_____   _____   _____
_____   _____   _____
_____   _____   _____
_____   _____   _____
_____   _____   _____
_____   _____   _____
_____   _____   _____
_____   _____   _____
_____   _____   _____

PSYCHOLOGICAL WARFARE:
Destroying the Power of Negative Words & Negative Thinking

You will need to drop every charge against these people and forgive them for the wrongful acts they committed against you.

THE POWER OF FORGIVENESS

With great emphasis, we find it necessary to discuss the importance of forgiving those who have wronged, violated, hurt, stole, manipulated, etc. you in any way. This is a defining moment for you; because this book is showing you there is a need for you to forgive your enemies. Forgiveness is making a conscious and deliberate decision to let go or release feelings of resentment, malice, hostility, anger or vengeance towards those who have hurt you. It is you choosing to release those negative feelings whether your enemies deserve it or not. Your choice of forgiveness allows God to judge the situation, that has wounded you to the core of your being. Today in this moment, make a conscious choice of forgiveness and say good bye to the past and hello to your future! Please pray the prayer of forgiveness on the next page.

PSYCHOLOGICAL WARFARE:
Destroying the Power of Negative Words & Negative Thinking

Prayer of Forgiveness

Father in the Name of Jesus Christ, I choose to forgive all those who have hurt, abandoned, violated, betrayed, stole, rejected, persecuted, lied, abused, falsely accused, and cursed me, in Jesus' Name. I forgive those who have not supported or loved me the way I have loved them. This day I choose to drop every charge against (call out every name you wrote on the previous pages)

_____
_____
_____
_____
_____
_____

I declare and decree I am free from the torment of unforgiveness. I choose to drop every charge, in Jesus Name. Now Lord Jesus, I ask You to forgive me of all my sins, restore and receive me back into Your Kingdom, in the Mighty Name of Jesus Christ, Amen!

PSYCHOLOGICAL WARFARE:
Destroying the Power of Negative Words & Negative Thinking

Chapter Three

THE STRONGHOLD OF NEGATIVISM

Have you ever been in a certain neighborhood, region or country, and felt a presence of darkness, or became confused and disoriented? Have you ever discerned an evil spirit controlling a specific group, city or nation? Have you ever witnessed a particular attitude or disposition upon a group or culture of people? If you answered yes to any of these questions, then you have seen the manifestation of a stronghold. A **"stronghold"** is a set pattern of thinking that is built upon the lies and deception of satan. It is a haven for demonic activity. It is a process where the enemy oppresses the mind of an individual to influence them to deviate from truth, and righteousness. The devil uses a traumatic situation to cause emotional hurt, and pain to be a gateway for his demonic spirits to lay a foundation of deception, by erecting a house of evil thoughts. He takes advantage of emotional hurts and disappointments by ministering

PSYCHOLOGICAL WARFARE:
Destroying the Power of Negative Words & Negative Thinking

lies through a spirit of unforgiveness, bringing evil thoughts and images to the mind of his victims.

The mind that is oppressed by the stronghold of negativism is bombarded with a continuous flow of negative thoughts, layered by negative beliefs. This is a <u>treacherous</u> stronghold because it deceives its victim and perpetuates negative thoughts to keep their mental state functioning in an unhealthy manner. People who are oppressed by negativism always speak about the negative issues of a matter; instead of the positive. They are pessimistic in their perception, and cannot see the good in a situation because of the spirit of negativism. The spirit of negativism positions itself at the gate of their mind, magnifying every problem and issue of negativity. Our mission in this chapter is to dismantle the stronghold of negativism.

Personally speaking, have you ever done something all your life and you thought it was right? Not only did you engage in this wrong, but your entire family did, also. However, when you read the Bible you

PSYCHOLOGICAL WARFARE:
Destroying the Power of Negative Words & Negative Thinking

discovered that your behavior patterns were contrary to the word of God; meaning you where operating wrongly and perhaps unrighteously, violating the statues of God. With acknowledgement of your sins, you still find yourself doing that personal practice, in spite of the word of God. This is a clear indication you are functioning with a stronghold. Remember a stronghold is a set pattern of thoughts causing one to believe his motives and methods are right and true. Actually the reality is, his thoughts have been erected out of a foundation of falsehood, through the deception of satan.

Ephesians 4:17-18

This I say therefore, and testify in the Lord, that ye henceforth walk not as other Gentiles walk, in the vanity of their mind. Having the understanding darkened, being alienated from the life of God through the ignorance that is in them, because of the blindness of their heart:

St. John 8:44

Ye are of your father the devil, and the lusts of your father ye will do. He was a murderer from the beginning, and abode not in the truth, because there is no truth in him. When he speaketh a lie, he speaketh of his own: for he is a liar, and the father of it.

PSYCHOLOGICAL WARFARE:
Destroying the Power of Negative Words & Negative Thinking

In order to strip and dismantle the functioning of this stronghold, we are challenged to uncover its demonic layers and demonic links that have built a fortress within the mind of the believer. These fortresses consist of negative thoughts, negative visions, negative vows, negative beliefs, negative desires, and negative behaviors. The true essence of psychological warfare opposes all thoughts, ideals, revelation, truth, and destiny that come from Almighty God. The negative stronghold protects all the negative activity that perpetuates the lies in the mind of the believer. This kind of stronghold keeps the mind in bondage and in a state of turmoil. The word of God gives us specific instruction when dealing with a stronghold and a strongman.

II Corinthians 10:4-6

(For the weapons of our warfare are not carnal, but mighty through God to the pulling down of strong holds;)
Casting down imaginations, and every high thing that exalteth itself against the knowledge of God, and bringing into captivity every thought to the obedience of Christ;
And having in a readiness to revenge all disobedience, when your obedience is fulfilled.

PSYCHOLOGICAL WARFARE:
Destroying the Power of Negative Words & Negative Thinking

In studying this passage, there are some <u>instructions</u> given to the believer when dealing with strongholds. Remember a **stronghold** is a fenced area of deception in the mind, that keeps a person thinking in a pattern that is contrary to the word of God. We shall examine this intricately in the scriptures.

- We have weapons that are spiritual, not carnal; these spiritual weapons assist us in conquering spiritual demons.

- We have power to pull down, demolish, and destroy strongholds through God.

- We can cast down imaginations, and theories, reasonings, false religions, erroneous teachings, and philosophies set forth to defy the knowledge of God.

- We can bring into captivity every thought to the obedience of Christ. This includes any thinking that is contrary to the purity and righteousness of God.

- We also must be ready to execute correction on all disobedience, when we are standing totally in a position of obedience.

PSYCHOLOGICAL WARFARE:
Destroying the Power of Negative Words & Negative Thinking

Matthew 12:25-29

And Jesus knew their thoughts, and said unto them, Every kingdom divided against itself is brought to desolation; and every city or house divided against itself shall not stand:
And if Satan cast out Satan, he is divided against himself; how shall then his kingdom stand?
And if I by Beelzebub cast out devils, by whom do your children cast them out? therefore they shall be your judges.
But if I cast out devils by the Spirit of God, then the kingdom of God is come unto you. Or else how can one enter into a strong man's house, and spoil his goods, except he first bind the strong man? and then he will spoil his house.

In this passage, the Lord Jesus Christ reveals to us His power over satan. He informs us that His authority is the only power authorized to cast out devils. Then He tells us that we can enter the strong man's house, the demonic territory of satan and plunder his goods; but first we must bind the strongman. In dealing with the **strongman,** the strongman is a power demon lodged in one's thought realm. It is the demon that sits at the gate of the mind, holding the stronghold in a position of power to invade the mind of an individual. It is positioned as a demonic gate keeper in the mind of a

PSYCHOLOGICAL WARFARE:
Destroying the Power of Negative Words & Negative Thinking

believer. This kind of gate keeper is evil and deceptive. Its purpose is to keep demonic thoughts flowing through the mind of the believer. This is why it is very crucial in the process of deliverance, for a person to recognize demonic negative thoughts, and identify the source of thought; in order to complete the experience of healing and deliverance in the mind. The strongman influences, leads, and controls by force: the thought, will, character, and behavior of an individual. It is liken unto a demonic agent invading the thought process of an individual to corrupt the mind with lies, untruths, and deception. Through the authority of Jesus Christ, we have power to invade satan's territory, nullify his evil activities, and take his goods. However, first, we must bind up the strongman and dismantle his stronghold. The scriptures prove to us satan's power is weak compared to the power of God! Are you ready to bind the strongman of negativism and destroy his stronghold?

PSYCHOLOGICAL WARFARE:
Destroying the Power of Negative Words & Negative Thinking

In conclusion, the remainder of this chapter is strategic in aiding you in the process of dismantling and destroying the stronghold of negativism. It is important for the believer to walk by faith and confront the negative thoughts arising in our minds. On the next few pages, we share with you, a process of deliverance to assist you in properly identifying and eradicating all signs, symptoms and manifestations of negativity in the mind. We also list the imps that must be called out in totally destroying the stronghold of negativism. Prepare for a deep inner soul cleansing from the stronghold of negativism, and your mind shall change permanently!

The Diagram on the next page is an example of how the Stronghold of Negativity can build demonic links in the mind, and open doors to other power demons. When power demons connect and link together they create demonic systems in the mind of the believer, which influences negatively the attitude, character, and behavior of a person.

PSYCHOLOGICAL WARFARE:
Destroying the Power of Negative Words & Negative Thinking

The Forming of a Demonic System

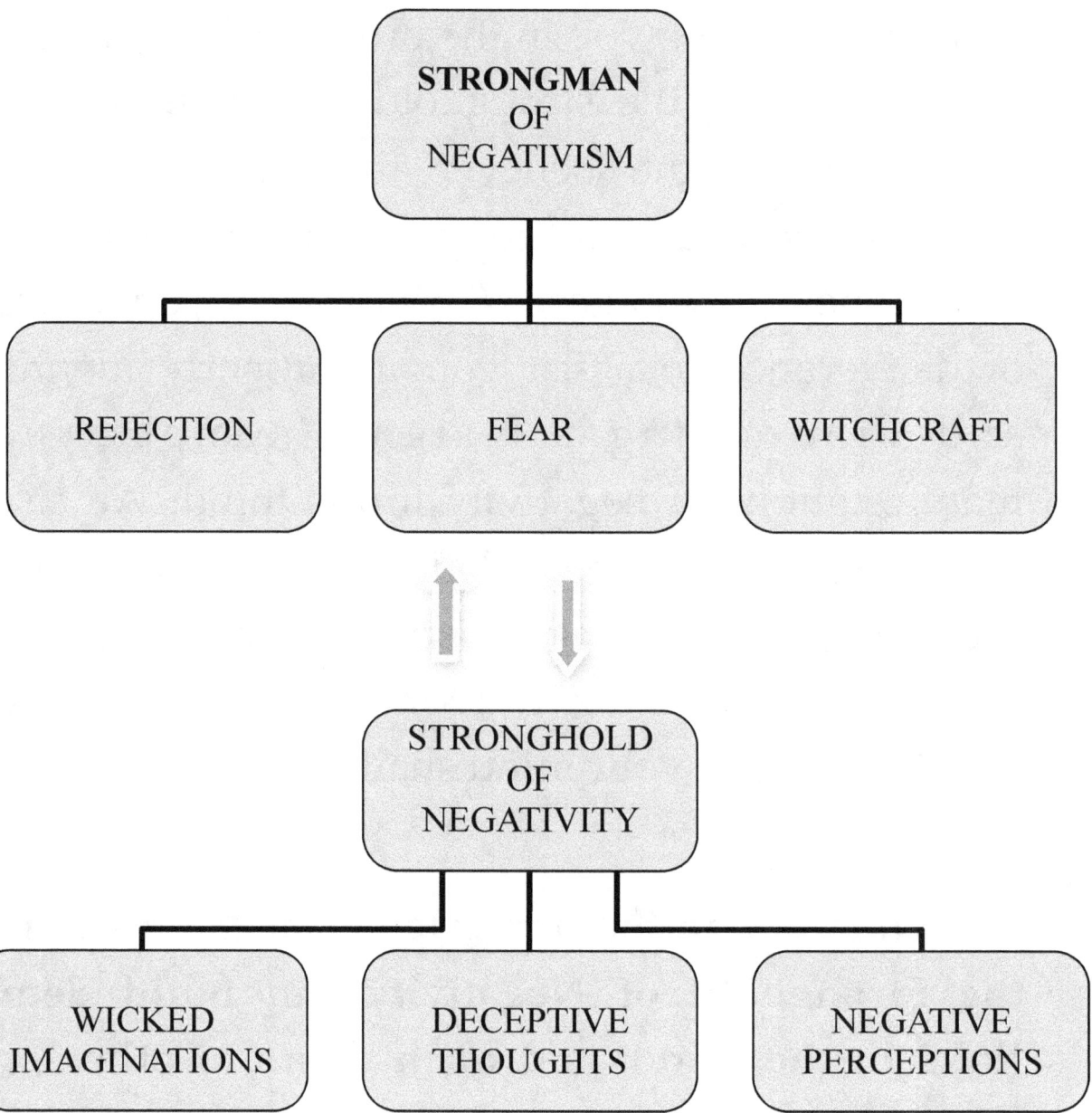

This is an example of how the spirit of negativity creates a **cycle of confusion** in the mind, to keep a person **distorted** in their thinking. The **strongman** is **negativism** and the other power demons joined as demonic links to form the demonic system!

Copyright © DR. CHARISSEE LEWIS, 2017

PSYCHOLOGICAL WARFARE:
Destroying the Power of Negative Words & Negative Thinking

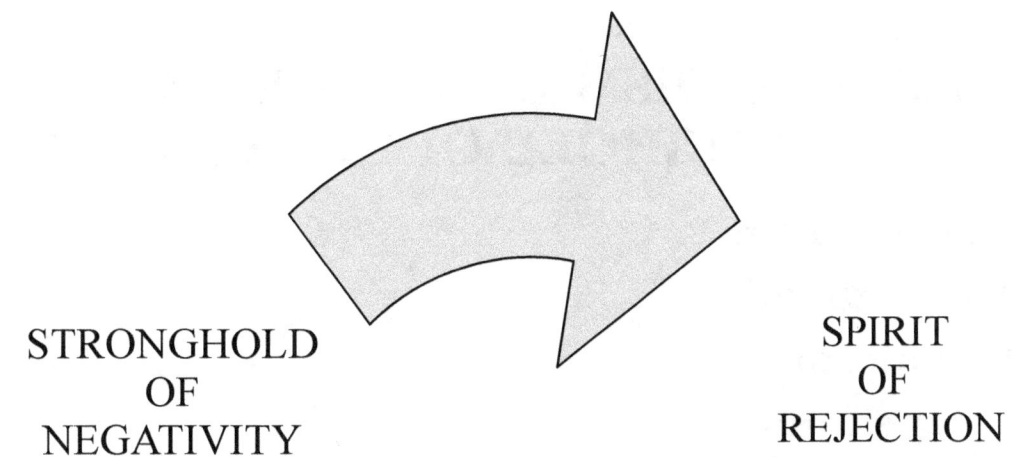

STRONGHOLD OF NEGATIVITY

SPIRIT OF REJECTION

SPIRIT OF FEAR

Cycle of Confusion

PSYCHOLOGICAL WARFARE:
Destroying the Power of Negative Words & Negative Thinking

KEYS TO DISMANTLE THE DEMONIC STRONGHOLD OF NEGATIVISM

- Recognition
- Identification
- Confession
- Repentance
- Deliverance
- Maintenance of Deliverance

1. **Recognition** – To acknowledge the existence, validity, authority, or genuineness; and admission, as of a fact.

2. **Identification** - Mainly unconscious process by which a person formulates a mental image of another person and then thinks, feels, and acts in a way which resembles this image.

3. **Confession** – An admission of guilt; the acknowledgement of sin.

4. **Repentance** – To feel sorry or regret, dissatisfaction over some past action, or intention.

5. **Deliverance** – A setting free; to rescue or release from demonic oppression and influence.

6. **Maintenance of Deliverance** – To remain in a state of freedom.

Copyright © DR. CHARISSEE LEWIS, 2017

PSYCHOLOGICAL WARFARE:
Destroying the Power of Negative Words & Negative Thinking

SIGNS, SYMPTOMS, & MANIFESTATIONS OF NEGATIVITY

Abnegate	Spirit of "No"	Critical Spirit
Refuse	Reject	Rejection
Disapprove	Refusal	Pessimistic
Non-consenting	Oppositional	Contrary
Disagreeing	Resistance	Hindrance
Defense Mechanism	Dissociation	Escapism
Defense Reaction	Fantasy	Withdrawal
Ego Mechanism	Rationalization	Abolish
Dispute	Veto	Pessimistic
Shake One's Head.	Not Admit	Pride
Disown	Disaffirm	Disavow
Abject	Abjure	Renounce
Retract	Revoke	Repudiate
Contradict	Refute	Nullify
Un-cheerfulness	Gloominess	Defeatism
Cynical	Retreatism	Unacceptance
Gloomy Outlook	Negative Attitude	Naysaying
Obtuseness	Gainsay	Gainsayer
Perverse	Cross	Backbiting
Talebearer	Poison Tongue	Vain Babbling
Fork Tongue	Viper Spirit	Negatory
Doubled Tongue.	Opposition	Revocation
Assert the Contrary	Contravene	Depreciate
Devalue	Emasculate	Dominance

Copyright © DR. CHARISSEE LEWIS, 2017

PSYCHOLOGICAL WARFARE:
Destroying the Power of Negative Words & Negative Thinking

SIGNS, SYMPTOMS, & MANIFESTATION OF NEGATIVITY
(Cont)

Defeatism	Deal Breaker	Disownment
Annulment	Flat Denial	Contention
Emphatic	Resistance	Two-Faced
Contrary Assertion	Offensive	Distorted
Repulse	Repugnance	Decline
Truce Breaker	Untruthful	Jealousy
Covenant Breaker	Undercurrent	Contest
Faultfinder	Equalizing	Negative Views
Lying spirits	Whisper Lies	Untruthful
Defiling Thoughts	Evil Imagination	Dishonor
Magnifying Wrongs	Entitlement	Hatred
Exposing Others Sins	Dislike	Disobedience
Hidden Jealousy	Revenge	Debate
Unforgiveness	Defiant	Manipulation
Witchcraft	Gossiper	Bitterness
Hidden Jealousy	Revenge	Hostility
Sabotage	Spirit of Strife	Judgmental
Distrust	Friction	Go Against
Aggressive Anger	Standing Against	Rebuttal
Noncooperation	Counter working	Head Wind
Indignation	Crosscurrent	Disaccord
Stiff Opposition	Stubbornness	Contest
Spiritual Collision	Tongue Clashing	Rivalry

PSYCHOLOGICAL WARFARE:
Destroying the Power of Negative Words & Negative Thinking

SIGNS, SYMPTOMS, & MANIFESTATION OF NEGATIVITY
(Cont)

- Sabotaging Purposes
- Bloody-Mindedness
- Character Deformation
- Cross-Purposes
- Strive Against
- Adversary
- Disrespect Authority
- Blood-Thirsty Spirits
- Enemy
- Struggle Against
- Dishonor
- Side Against
- Usurp Authority
- Demonic Thinking
- Sorcery
- Destructive Spirits
- Negative Speaking
- Suspicion
- Fear of Rejection
- Wrong Thoughts
- Wrong Behavior
- Distance
- Moodiness
- Obstructionism
- Argumentative
- Dissension
- Latent Hostility
- Confrontational
- Unfriendly
- Antagonistic
- Unsympathetic
- Clash With
- Butt Heads
- At War With
- Conniving
- Familiar Spirits
- Shrewd Spirits
- Confusion
- Lust for Power
- Seducing Spirits
- Resistance
- Wrong Emotions
- Challenging
- Rolling Eyes
- Bad Attitude
- Sighing

PSYCHOLOGICAL WARFARE:
Destroying the Power of Negative Words & Negative Thinking

SIGNS, SYMPTOMS, & MANIFESTATION OF NEGATIVITY(Cont)

Fear of Change	Noncompliance
Hopelessness	Cunning
Hard to Hear	Refuse to Listen
Suicide	Cunning Craftiness
The Spirit of Offense	On the Defense
Selfishness	Scattered Thinking
Irrational	Jezebellic Spirits
Hatred of Men	Hatred of Women
Combative	Delusional
Hatred of Authority	Insecure
Avoidance Mechanism	Fragmented Thinking
Negative Thinking	Deflecting Conversations
Manipulation through Pity	Faultfinding
Anti-Submissiveness	Emasculating Men
The Spirit of Witchcraft	The Spirit of Wizardry
Controlling Powers	Infusing One's Thoughts
Emotional Abuse	Deflecting
Projection of Anger	Clever Trickery
Verbal Abuse	Mental Abuse
Narcissism	Delusional
Throw the Rock; Hid the Hand	
Sociological Adjustive Reaction	

- Please follow the process on page 53 and pray this prayer:

PSYCHOLOGICAL WARFARE:
Destroying the Power of Negative Words & Negative Thinking

Dismantling the Stronghold of Negativism

Father in the Name of Jesus Christ, Lord I come to You seeking Your forgiveness. I have been spiritually blind and spiritually deaf, by the deception of the enemy. Lord, You said in Your word whatever I bind on earth is bound in heaven, whatever I loosed on earth is loosed in heaven, according to **Matthew 18:18**, in Jesus' Name. I bind up the strongman of negativism and all his demonic links and layers that have infiltrated my soul; my mind, my will, my emotion, my imagination, my memory, and my intellect, in Jesus' Name. Lord, I dismantle every demon that is associated with this strongman. I cast out the spirit of indecisiveness, confusion, aggravation, frustration, revenge, rage, murder, bitterness, violence, malice, mayhem, deceit, distrust, anger, fear, hatred, un-forgiveness, doubt, skepticism, disillusionment, negative beliefs, negative vows, negative thoughts, negative words, stubbornness, witchcraft, rebellion, idolatry, sorcery, gossip, tale bearing, lust, perversion, fear of hurt, jealousy, fear of

PSYCHOLOGICAL WARFARE:
Destroying the Power of Negative Words & Negative Thinking

Dismantling the Stronghold of Negativism (con't)

disappointment, fear of rejection, rejection, self-rejection, pride, mental anguish, mental stress, low self-esteem, low self-worth, and any other spirit that is unknown to me but known to God, in Jesus' Name. I cast you out of every area of my life, in Jesus' Name. Satan, I rebuke your demonic layers and links out of my mind and I receive the mind of Christ, in the Name of Jesus Christ. No longer, will I be overwhelmed by negative thoughts, and images of tragedy in my mind, in Jesus' Name. I loose the love of Jesus Christ, peace, longsuffering, goodness, temperance, meekness, gentleness, patience, the pure gifts of the Holy Spirit, the Spirit of counsel, the Spirit of might, the Spirit of knowledge, the Spirit of life, the Spirit of wisdom, and the Spirit of prophecy, in Jesus' Name. For God has not given me the spirit of fear, but of power, of love, and of a sound mind, according to II Timothy 1:7. I thank You, Lord, for healing my mind and my entire soul, in Jesus' Name. Lord Jesus, I

PSYCHOLOGICAL WARFARE:
Destroying the Power of Negative Words & Negative Thinking

Dismantling the Stronghold of Negativism (con't)

repent of pride, I shall walk before You with a meek and contrite spirit, in Jesus' Name. I will no longer fear what the future may bring, in Jesus' Name. I have a healthy spiritual mind, in Jesus' Name. I shall walk by faith and not by sight; I am a new creation in Christ Jesus, in Jesus' Name. I will achieve my destiny and walk in purpose, and complete my mandate in the entire universe, in Jesus' Name. I proclaim Jesus Christ as Lord of my life, and I am happy to be a servant, free in my spirit, my soul and my body, in Jesus Name. I declare and decree, this day I am made whole, in the Mighty Name of Jesus Christ, Amen!

Philippians 2:5

Let this mind be in you, which was also in Christ Jesus:

PSYCHOLOGICAL WARFARE:
Destroying the Power of Negative Words & Negative Thinking

Chapter Four

THE POWER OF THE TONGUE: WORD CURSES

Have you ever said something that you wanted to take back? Or regret what you have spoken to someone? Of course, you have! Many of us have imagined scenarios in the deep corridors of our mind that were too defiling to mention. One of the greatest attribute of the mind is that no one knows your thoughts, unless the Holy Spirit reveals it to them through the gifts of revelation; or your thoughts can be revealed through your speech.   Unlike the mind, when the tongue speaks it reveals thoughts within the heart and mind of man. The tongue is so powerful it has the ability to create or to destroy. It can build up or it can tear down. It has the ability to create or destroy; this is why it is essential for us to use our tongue as an instrument of righteousness. The bible confirms this fact, according to the book of Proverbs,

PSYCHOLOGICAL WARFARE:
Destroying the Power of Negative Words & Negative Thinking

Proverbs 18:21

Death and life are in the power of the tongue: and they that love it shall eat the fruit thereof.

Death and life can be determined by the power of the tongue, and when we learn how to use the power of the tongue, wisely; we shall live life in a new dimension of faith, because of what we have spoken secretly and publicly. In other words, we shall become a recipient of what we speak with our tongue. The tongue can be defiling and the initiator of trouble. It cannot be tamed; the bible warns us about the power of the tongue. The scriptures below reveal the nature of the tongue.

James 3:3-6

Behold, we put bits in the horses' mouth, that they may obey us; and we turn about their whole body.

Behold also the ships, which though *they be* so great, and *are* driven of fierce winds, yet are they turned about with a very small helm, whithersoever the governor listeth.

Even so the tongue is a little member, and boasteth great things. Behold, how great a matter a little fire kindleth!

Copyright © DR. CHARISSEE LEWIS, 2017

PSYCHOLOGICAL WARFARE:
Destroying the Power of Negative Words & Negative Thinking

And the tongue is a fire, a world of iniquity: so is the tongue among our members, that it defileth the whole body, and setteth on fire the course of nature; and it is set on fire of hell.

These scriptures indicate to us the tongue is little, but it has the ability to ignite a fire. It can create cycles of iniquity in the life of human beings when it is not sanctified. The tongue can set the whole course of life on the fire of hell, according to James 3:6. This scripture is referring to the violent passions, anger, rage, and wrath that pertain to vile language which comes from the tongue. Therefore, as Christians, we are admonished to sanctify, and control our tongues. We should be mindful of what we speak and become discipline to not say everything that comes to our minds. We need healthy spiritual minds to speak words that are appropriate to life's situations. We have a responsibility to speak wisely and righteously to one another.

James 3:7-8
For every kind of beasts, and of birds, and of serpents, and of things in the sea, is tamed, and hath been tamed of mankind:

PSYCHOLOGICAL WARFARE:
Destroying the Power of Negative Words & Negative Thinking

But the tongue can no man tame; it is an unruly evil, full of deadly poison.

The value of speaking the right words can give us favor with people in high places and open new doors for us. Often times, we are remembered by what we say, and how we respond to different situations in our lives. Our words are so powerful; speaking good or evil words has the ability to reach the core of a person's soul. There are negative consequences to face when speaking evil; we get ourselves in trouble with God and others. Unfortunately, people do not realize the power God has given us with our tongues. The scriptures above tell us all species of beasts has been tamed by mankind, but the tongue of man cannot be tamed; it can only be controlled through salvation and sanctification. We abuse our authority as Christians by speaking evil against one another; sometimes knowingly and unknowingly, invoking curses. A **word curse** is a word spoken over, to or about someone that activate demons to cause harm or injury to come upon the person, it was spoken over, to or about. A word curse looses a spirit of torment with it,

PSYCHOLOGICAL WARFARE:
Destroying the Power of Negative Words & Negative Thinking

to bring mental anguish with the spoken curse. Word curses create havoc in the lives of people. It produces an obstacle in the spiritual realm that must be destroyed in order for a person to experience victory in that area of their life and defeat the word curse that has been spoken against them. The bible warns us about speaking evil, and cursing others. These scriptures share with us the ungodly use of the tongue in **James 3:9-12**; they also give us four comparisons.

James 3:9-12

Therewith bless we God, even the Father; and therewith curse we men, which are made after the similitude of God.

Out of the same mouth proceedeth blessings and cursings. My brethren, these things ought not so to be.

Doth a fountain send forth at the same place sweet water and bitter?

Can the fig tree, my brethren, bear olive berries? either a vine, figs? so can no fountain both yield salt water and fresh.

PSYCHOLOGICAL WARFARE:
Destroying the Power of Negative Words & Negative Thinking

Four Comparisons Concerning the Tongue

1. A fountain cannot produce sweet water and bitter water at the same time.
2. A fig tree cannot produce olive trees.
3. A vine cannot produce figs.
4. The ocean cannot produce sweet water.

As you can see there is no other creature in nature that can compare to the double use of the tongue. According to the scriptures the tongue, is able to cause an individual to speak blessings and curses out of the same mouth. We must guard the words that come out of our mouths! We should not want to be believers who are guilty of speaking blessings and curses out of our mouths!

James 3:13

Who is a wise man and endued with knowledge among you? Let him shew out of a good conversation his works with meekness of wisdom.

Ephesians 4:31-32

Let all bitterness, and wrath and anger, and clamor and evil speaking, be put away from you, with all malice:

Copyright © DR. CHARISSEE LEWIS, 2017

PSYCHOLOGICAL WARFARE:
Destroying the Power of Negative Words & Negative Thinking

And be ye kind one to another, tenderhearted, forgiving one another, even as God for Christ's sake hath forgiven you.

James 4:11

Speak not evil one of another, brethren. He that speaketh evil of his brother,
and judgeth his brother, speaketh evil of the law, and judgeth the law: but if thou judge the law, thou art not a doer of the law, but a judge.

The bible admonishes us to speak wise words. A person who can bridle his own tongue is wise. A person who is wise can also speak wise words with meekness and is qualified to teach others. Wise words are words that reveal the authority of Jesus Christ. They give life, and open the mind to receive new revelation knowledge. They create an atmosphere of love and security. These are words that are appropriate, forcible, comforting, gracious, inspiring, pleasant, kind, and unforgettable. Can you find these words in the scriptures, concerning speaking wise words? In order to change your words, you will need to study and meditate on the word of God to break up the ancient demons and negative words purposed to invade your heart and soul.

PSYCHOLOGICAL WARFARE:
Destroying the Power of Negative Words & Negative Thinking

THE SPIRITUAL ASPECT OF WORD CURSES

There is a Spirit world that we must become acquainted with, as believers. In understanding the Spirit world, the words we speak in the natural world affects what occurs in Spirit world. There is a spiritual reaction which correlates to our natural actions. The scriptures below prove to us there is a spirit world that exists, because God is a Spirit; and the words that He speaks are spirit and life. The bible tells us in the book of John,

John 4:24

God is a Spirit: and they that worship him must worship him in spirit and in truth.

John 6:63

It is the spirit that quickeneth; the flesh profiteth nothing: the words that I speak unto you, they are spirit and *they* are life.

With that being said, words are powerful and they have the ability to create and destroy. Therefore, it is essential for us to speak the right words in the right

PSYCHOLOGICAL WARFARE:
Destroying the Power of Negative Words & Negative Thinking

season; most importantly, we must speak what God is saying concerning a person or situation. The scripture below reveals to us that death and life is determined by the power of the tongue, and when we use the tongue rightly; we can experience a fruitful life because of what we speak. Frankly, our words have a great influence on the life we live, because spiritually speaking they affect our entire environment.

Proverbs 18:21

Death and life are in the power of the tongue: and they that love it shall eat the fruit thereof.

Now that you understand the words we speak, really have a spiritual effect on our lives; we can move into deeper knowledge of understanding the results and spiritual dimensions of negative words. As believers, we must realize that positive and negative words have a direct effect on our emotions and they lay dormant deep within our subconscious mind influencing decisions we make on a daily basis. These words can motivate us to do good or evil. Therefore, negative

PSYCHOLOGICAL WARFARE:
Destroying the Power of Negative Words & Negative Thinking

words and word curses can stifle the progress of anyone who is unaware of verbal attacks. When people constantly speak evil of a person; or are opinionated critically and negatively about a person: it creates a flaming dart in the realm of the spirit which becomes a weapon against the person they are attacking verbally. The moment we speak evil or negatively about a person, a demonic spirit is assign to our words to bring to life the negative evil words, we have spoken. This too, is the forming of a word curse. As believers, we must be cautious that the enemy does not use our mouths as an instrument of unrighteousness, speaking curses upon our brothers and sisters in Christ, and even people we do not know. Too often, we are victimized by slanderous words, negative opinions, and false accusations from the mouth of love ones and strangers. The Body of Christ is suffering from negative words we have spoken against one another. It is time for the people of God to become accountable and responsible for speaking negatively against one another. The bible tells us how the Lord feels about activities involving

PSYCHOLOGICAL WARFARE:
Destroying the Power of Negative Words & Negative Thinking

negative speaking according to Proverbs,

Proverbs 6:16-19

These six things doth the LORD hate: yea, seven are an abomination unto him: A proud look, a lying tongue, and hands that shed innocent blood. An heart that deviseth wicked imaginations, feet that be swift in running to mischief, A false witness that speaketh lies, and he that soweth discord among brethren.

The Lord hates:
1. A proud look
2. A lying tongue
3. Hands that shed innocent blood
4. A heart that deviseth wicked imaginations
5. Feet that be swift in running to mischief
6. A false witness that speaketh lies
7. He that soweth discord among brethren

Many times, when a person is speaking against someone; one or more of these activities are involved. We cannot continue to superimpose our negative opinions about someone on others, and think God is not going to judge us. Negative words and word curses hurt the people we talk about; and ultimately

PSYCHOLOGICAL WARFARE:
Destroying the Power of Negative Words & Negative Thinking

they also hurt the person who is speaking the curse. It is time to change our conversations and build up one another and not tear others down.

In summary, verbal attacks are a conglomerate of slanderous evil words spoken by a person or a group of people repeatedly. These words collectively form an arrow, dart, or weapon in the spirit world to attack the person who is being talked about: the weapon is purposed to bring pain to the heart, mind, or physical body of that person. It is a treacherous attack because many times, it comes from people who say they love you and whom you may consider as family. This is why it is imperative for us to dismiss ourselves from all negative words, psychic prayers, dominate opinions, false accusations, infusing thoughts of others, and word curses spoken to us, against us, about us; seen or unseen; heard or unheard; known or unknown. We must disallow any verbal attacks from operating in our lives. We have to use our authority to close up, seal up, and shut up all satanic gates, open doors, and demonic portals that may be opened in the

PSYCHOLOGICAL WARFARE:
Destroying the Power of Negative Words & Negative Thinking

realm of the spirit. Even if our fore-fathers engaged in abominable practices that opened demonic portals, demonic gates, and evil judgments; we must still confront these generational sins, and generational iniquities through prayer and intercession. This is a necessity in destroying the power of negative words!

In the next few pages, we provided information from the Word of God concerning the tongue to assist you in identifying where you need to tame your tongue. We also designed a series of exercises to help you break up the word curses that may be oppressing you.

PSYCHOLOGICAL WARFARE:
Destroying the Power of Negative Words & Negative Thinking

I. Breaking Word Curses:

- In your childhood, was there any words or statements spoken to you that hurt your feelings, or scarred your emotions?

- Did your parents, siblings or relatives screamed, yelled, or called you bad names, when they became angry with you?

- Did a teacher ever call you names for not learning or understanding what was being taught?

- In past relationships or friendships, were you called out of your name?

- Have you ever been involved in a verbally abusive, mentally abusive, emotionally abusive, or physically abusive relationship?

- Were you teased and ridiculed as a child?

- Are you presently offended by something that was said about you or to you, that hurt your feelings?

PSYCHOLOGICAL WARFARE:
Destroying the Power of Negative Words & Negative Thinking

Reader, we have written some common words that can hurt people feelings, causing feelings of inadequacy, a poor self-image, and emotional damage especially when spoken sarcastically, through ridicule, anger, or spoken repeatedly.

Please be honest and check what appears to you, so you can began your process of inner healing and deliverance. The words and phrases listed are words that have been spoken to you or words you have spoken to others. Either way, these words and phrases must be uprooted out of your conscious and subconscious.

PSYCHOLOGICAL WARFARE:
Destroying the Power of Negative Words & Negative Thinking

Check what applies to you:

Word Curses

flunky	thot	demon
you are a disgrace	buck eyes	frog eyes
cock eyed	buck tooth	nosey
flat chested	bertha but	flat but
reject	big dummy	stupid
shorty	gumpy	airhead
duh….	dumb-dumb	whitie
hunky	nigga	nigger
blackie	high-yellow	nappy head
but hole	dumb ……	big cow
ugly	ugly cow	chimp
black monkey	monkey	black dog
hoe	whore	slut
sack chaser	you po	poor
big head	bow legs	snag a tooth
get your tail…	I hate you	you're stupid
sybil	you can't read	butch
you can't count	you're cursed	dike
can't do nothing	shut up	fag
faggot	roach	you stink
you're fat	you're too fat	witch
you're evil	old hag	crack
suck my…..	lazy	gold digger
half breed	who asked you	heifer

Copyright © DR. CHARISSEE LEWIS, 2017

PSYCHOLOGICAL WARFARE:
Destroying the Power of Negative Words & Negative Thinking

Word Curses
(cont)

I'll beat your but
b…ch
too old
motherf…….
big gut
you smell
young n dumb
I'll kill you
black sheep
I'm ashamed of you
re-tard
control freak
are you slow
bald head
clumsy
you're crazy
you don't know nothing
you smell like dodo
good for nothing
you're stupid
you big dummy
you're wearing those rags again
you will never have nothing
you think you know it all

you will never be nothing
you will never have nothing
you have a mind of a baby
don't nobody want you
nobody likes you
snag-a-tooth
smell my butt

PSYCHOLOGICAL WARFARE:
Destroying the Power of Negative Words & Negative Thinking

Now that you have identified the word curses, you must renounce these negative words and phrases that have scarred your emotions.

For example, you can say, *"I rebuke and renounce the power of negative word curses, I refute the word dummy and the evil spirits that is associated with this word, I rebuke its hold on my life and any hurt or pain that is associated with this negative word." I disallow these negative words to influence and infiltrate my thoughts. I strip these words of their power to operate in my life. I renounce and denounce these words from their ability to re-arrange my life, in Jesus Name.*

PSYCHOLOGICAL WARFARE:
Destroying the Power of Negative Words & Negative Thinking

The Process of Inner Healing & Deliverance

- ➤ You may manifest in this portion of the inner healing and deliverance section, so keep your tissue and disposal bag close.

- ➤ It is a normal practice during this portion of ministry to purge, spit, cough, yawn, and release mucus or waste from your body. The demonic spirits must be evicted from your body.

- ➤ Be honest with yourself and God; do not be afraid to confront what is deep within you.

- ➤ Now go back through the list, perhaps there is something you overlooked. Allow the Holy Spirit to speak to you concerning some words that are not listed.

Now that you have completed, the renunciation process you are ready to proceed into a deeper realm of deliverance. Stay prayerful and truthful with yourself! The Lord already knows where we need inner healing and deliverance.

PSYCHOLOGICAL WARFARE:
Destroying the Power of Negative Words & Negative Thinking

Part II. Mouth Demons:

Demons that attack your mouth, they alter, degrade, defile and miscommunicate what we say.

- *Choose what applies to you:*

__foul mouth
__sarcasm
__peeping & muttering
__statements of fear
__name calling
__stammering
__repeating statements
__words of doubt
__prideful statements
__flattery
__wicked words
__seductive words
__critical statements
__dirty mouth
__sucking thumb/fingers
__instigate
__double tongue
__words of rejection
__false accusations
__verbal pauses inappropriately
__not able to say true feelings
__words of fear
__sexual innuendoes
__false witness bearing lies
__harsh critical words
__bringing up the past
__flirtatious comments

__profanity
__tale bearer
__back biter
__rotten teeth
__whispering
__teeth missing
__mouth sores
__sore gums
__dirty jokes
__mockery
__instigate
__evil speaking
__boasting
__telling secrets
__mocking others
__evil words
__tale-bearing
__oral habits
__persecution
__lying
__word curses
__gossip
__hissing spirits
__bad breathe
__slang
__words of defeat
__words of negativity

Copyright © DR. CHARISSEE LEWIS, 2017

PSYCHOLOGICAL WARFARE:
Destroying the Power of Negative Words & Negative Thinking

Part II. Mouth Demons: (con't)

__ words of judgment
__ belittling statements
__ words of ridicule
__ telling lies
__ affinity for gossip
__ words of resentment
__ words of envy
__ words of jealousy
__ foul breathe
__ words of contention
__ words of strife
__ belittling others to exalt self
__ words of abuse
__ improper words
__ words of allurement
__ words spoken to entice
__ words that repeat others
__ words of hatred
__ word curses
__ words of witchcraft
__ words that cause embarrassment for others
__ words of spoken out of a wicked imagination
__ words that cause embarrassment for others

Copyright © DR. CHARISSEE LEWIS, 2017

PSYCHOLOGICAL WARFARE:
Destroying the Power of Negative Words & Negative Thinking

Twelve Characteristics of the Tongue

1. A little member
2. Boasts great things
3. Is a fire
4. A world of iniquity
5. It defiles the whole body
6. Sets a fire the course of nature
7. It is untamable
8. An unruly evil
9. Full of deadly poison
10. Used to bless God and curse men
11. Capable of good conversation
12. Capable of bitter strife

Copyright © DR. CHARISSEE LEWIS, 2017

PSYCHOLOGICAL WARFARE:
Destroying the Power of Negative Words & Negative Thinking

Sixteen Kinds of Tongues

1. Backbiting tongue ....Proverbs 25:23
2. Death and Life tongue......................Proverbs 18:21
3. Deceitful tongue...............................Psalms 120:2
4. False tongue.....................................Psalms 120:3
5. Flattering tongue..............................Psalms 5:9
6. Froward tongue.................................Proverbs 10:31
7. Healthy tongue..................................Proverbs 12:18
8. Lying tongue.....................................Psalms 109:2
9. Naughty tongue.................................Proverbs 17:4
10. Perverse tongue................................Proverbs 17:20
11. Proud tongue....................................Psalms 12:3
12. Soft tongue.......................................Proverbs 25:15
13. Stammering tongue...........................Isaiah 28:11;33:19
14. Viper's tongue...................................Job 20:16
15. Wholesome tongue............................Proverbs 10:31
16. Wise Tongue.....................................James 3:13

Copyright © DR. CHARISSEE LEWIS, 2017

PSYCHOLOGICAL WARFARE:
Destroying the Power of Negative Words & Negative Thinking

Scriptures Concerning Wise Words:

1. Appropriate
Proverbs 25:11
A word fitly spoken is like apples of gold in pictures of silver.

2. Comforting
Isaiah 50:4
The Lord God hath given me the tongue of the learned, that I should know how to speak a word in season to him that is weary: he wakeneth morning by morning, he wakeneth mine ear to hear as the learned.

3. Forcible
Job 6:25
How forcible are right words! But what doth your arguing reprove?

4. Gracious
Ecclesiastes 10:12
The words of a wise man's mouth are gracious; but the lips of a fool will swallow up himself.

5. Inspiring and Unforgettable
Ecclesiastes 12:11
The words of the wise *are* as goads, and as nails fastened *by* the masters of assemblies, *which* are given from one shepherd.

6. Pleasant
Proverbs 16:24
Pleasant words *are as* an honeycomb, sweet to the soul, and health to the bones.

PSYCHOLOGICAL WARFARE:
Destroying the Power of Negative Words & Negative Thinking

Deliverance from Demons that Affect the Mouth

Father in the Name of Jesus Christ, I come to You with a repentance heart seeking Your forgiveness. Lord I admit, I am guilty of allowing evil mouth demons to influence my conversations. Lord, I ask that You cleanse my heart from the darkness of satan, in Jesus' Name. Lord, please uproot from my heart the weeds of unrighteous that would cause me to speak the wrong things, in Jesus' Name. Lord, I want to be purified in my heart from the wickedness of cursing, using profanity, negative speaking, and word curses, in Jesus' Name. Father, I am seeking a change in my mindset and my conversations, in Jesus' Name. Deliver me from the embarrassment of mouth demons; I cancel every generational curse that causes me to have no discretion over what I speak, in Jesus' Name. I rebuke the backbiting tongue, the deceitful tongue, the false tongue, the flattering tongue, the forward tongue, the lying tongue, the naughty tongue, the perverse tongue, the proud tongue, the stammering tongue, and the viper's tongue and I loose an healthy tongue and a wholesome

PSYCHOLOGICAL WARFARE:
Destroying the Power of Negative Words & Negative Thinking

Deliverance from Demons that Affect the Mouth (con't)

tongue, in Jesus' Name. I bind every foul spirit of (name out loud all the demons you checked) _____. I loose godly conversations, temperance, wise words, words that are spirit and life, in Jesus' Name. Lord, let my words be fitly spoken like apples of gold in pictures of silver, according to **Proverbs 25:11,** in Jesus' Name. Let me have spiritual conversation on a daily basis, because the mouth of a righteous man is a well of life, according to **Proverbs 10:11,** in Jesus' Name. Father God, I do not want to speak curses out of my mouth, in Jesus' Name. I want my mouth to be use by You, Father God. Holy Spirit, help me to walk in righteousness and speak the right words at the right time, in Jesus' Name. I want to help my brothers and sisters and not hurt them with the words that come out of my mouth, in Jesus' Name. Lord now I understand that negative speaking can lead to word curses; and word curses create weapons against others in the spirit world. I repent for this act

PSYCHOLOGICAL WARFARE:
Destroying the Power of Negative Words & Negative Thinking

Deliverance from Demons that Affect the Mouth (con't)

of allowing my mouth to speak words that caused curses to come upon the people I truly love, and from this day forward I will be mindful of the words I speak, in Jesus' Name. I will not be quick to opinionate, criticize, and judge the actions, and behaviors of others, in Jesus' Name. I will assume the posture of prayer and intercession that I may stay free and clear of sin; and committing one of the six sins that You hate and seven that are an abomination to you, in Jesus' Name. Thank You, Father God for new conversations, new wisdom, a new mindset, and a new level of love that will stop me from speaking evil of others, in Jesus' Name, Amen.

PSYCHOLOGICAL WARFARE:
Destroying the Power of Negative Words & Negative Thinking

DESTROYING NEGATIVITY

Copyright © DR. CHARISSEE LEWIS, 2017

PSYCHOLOGICAL WARFARE:
Destroying the Power of Negative Words & Negative Thinking

PSYCHOLOGICAL WARFARE:
Destroying the Power of Negative Words & Negative Thinking

Chapter Five

MIND BATTLES: DESTROYING NEGATIVE THINKING

Have you ever walked into a room or a crowd and felt that you did not belong there? Have you ever misplaced something and thought someone took it or moved it? Have you thought someone you knew was ignoring you; when the person never saw you? These are examples of common dilemmas people experience everyday; they are brief scenarios of mind battles. The mind is an important organ to the function of humanity. It gives us the ability to think, and it opens our understanding to take action. We know satan's aim is to attack human beings by any means necessary; and to stop us from walking in the will of God. He causes warfare in the mind, and uses the mind as a <u>battleground</u> to bring confusion and distractions to the thought life of the believer. He also uses strongholds to blind and bind the thoughts of the

PSYCHOLOGICAL WARFARE:
Destroying the Power of Negative Words & Negative Thinking

believer. Satan comes to dispute and argue with us mentally by constantly speaking words of negativity, words of accusation, and words of deception that are contrary to the word of God, these kinds of words create battles in the mind. A **mind battle** is conflict in the mind. It entails a negative thought trying to bombard truth in the mind of the believer. The battle of the mind causes psychological warfare; where the soul of a person is bound by demonic oppression, through attacks on the mind. In chapter three, we discussed how the stronghold of negativism is able to cunningly infiltrate the thoughts of the mind. Through the stronghold of negativism, the devil is able to permeate the carnal mind with defiling thoughts. He uses mind idolatry, and mind blinding spirits to perpetuate mental oppression. The carnal mind is a gateway for negative thinking, and it leads to death.

Romans 8:5-8

For they that are after the flesh do mind the things of the flesh; but they that are after the Spirit the things of the Spirit.
For to be carnally minded is death; but to be spiritually minded is life and peace.

PSYCHOLOGICAL WARFARE:
Destroying the Power of Negative Words & Negative Thinking

Because the carnal mind is enmity against God: for it is not subject to the law of God, neither indeed can be.
So then they that are in the flesh cannot please God.

The purpose of satan's attack involving negative thinking is to distract, detour, dissuade, and to dispattern us from achieving our true destiny. He is relentless in his opposition of harassment, and torment. Ultimately, he wants to destroy our minds, through the stronghold of negative thinking. It is important for us to keep our mental faculties functioning in a healthy manner. Satan is constantly trying to gain new ground in our thought life. We can not allow his wicked thoughts to linger in our minds. The bible tells us the importance of having right thoughts. Our thoughts should reflect the nature of Christ. To ensure we have thoughts that are pleasing to God; we must transform our mind from the carnal mind to the spiritual mind. We have to develop the mind of Christ. Let's examine the scriptures concerning the mind of Christ. The scripture informs us; in order to know the mind of the Lord and to be instructed of the Lord, we must have the mind of

Copyright © DR. CHARISSEE LEWIS, 2017

PSYCHOLOGICAL WARFARE:
Destroying the Power of Negative Words & Negative Thinking

Christ. As believers, when we give our lives to Christ, we do not automatically have the mind of Christ; it takes time for our minds to be renewed by the Spirit of God. During this process of renewal of the mind, satan will create continuous battles to discourage believers from receiving the full manifestation of the mind of Christ. It is important for us to identify the condition of our minds, and think positive thoughts while going through the spiritual renewal process of the mind.

Philippians 4:8

Finally, brethren, whatsoever things are true, whatsoever things *are* honest, whatsoever things *are* just, whatsoever things *are* pure, whatsoever things *are* lovely, whatsoever things *are* of good report; if *there be* any virtue, and if there be any praise, think on these things.

I Corinthians 2:11

For who hath known the mind of the Lord, that he may instruct him? But we have the mind of Christ.

Philippians 2:5

Let this mind be in you which was also in Christ Jesus:

PSYCHOLOGICAL WARFARE:
Destroying the Power of Negative Words & Negative Thinking

To have the mind of Christ, means to have a mindset of humility. The word humility means the absence of pride or self-assertion. When Jesus Christ walked the earth, He laid aside His divine form and made Himself of no reputation, even though He is **God**. The scriptures tell us He took on the form of a servant and became obedient unto death.

Philippians 2:6-8

Who, being in the form of God, thought it not robbery to be equal with God: But made himself of no reputation, and took upon him the form of a servant, and was made in the likeness of men:
And being found in fashion as a man, he humbled himself, and became obedient unto death, even the death of the cross.

As believers, we too, must take on the mind of Christ and become like Jesus Christ, as we walk in destiny. We too, must become obedient and die to the old thought patterns of the flesh. **Humility** is an essential quality and intricate part of the spiritual renewal process of the mind. It allows us to yield to God's will for our mind, and remove the old unregenerated thought patterns of the mind.

PSYCHOLOGICAL WARFARE:
Destroying the Power of Negative Words & Negative Thinking

Romans 12:2

And be not conformed to this world: but be ye transformed by the renewing of your mind, that ye may prove what is that good, and acceptable, and perfect, will of God.

Ephesians 4:21-23

If so be ye have heard him, and have been taught by him,
as the truth is in Jesus:
That ye put off concerning the former conversation the old man, which is corrupt according to the deceitful lusts; And be renewed in the spirit of your mind; And that ye put on the new man, which after God is created in righteousness and true holiness.

We must denounce the worldly mentality, which causes us to behave in the *old man* which is the spirit and nature of the the devil. Through the process of mind renewal, we must allow God to transform our heart and mind. This transformation requires a process of patience and time. The Lord wants us to be renewed in the spirit of our mind. This means we have to be renewed in the attitude and disposition of our mind. We are admonished to renounce the old desires, old habits, old conversations, and old behaviors of the flesh, such as vanity, and lusts; and to

PSYCHOLOGICAL WARFARE:
Destroying the Power of Negative Words & Negative Thinking

put on the new man and learn of Christ. He wants us to develop a spiritual mind. A spiritual mind is a mind <u>renewed</u>, <u>influenced</u>, and <u>motivated</u> by the Spirit of God. It is a mind that is Christ-centered, which causes believers to live our whole lives in submission to the laws of the Spirit. A spiritual mind ignites us to pursue a life in the Kingdom of God. A spiritual mind is life and peace, **Romans 8:6.** God has given us a method to achieve the spiritual mind; it is through meditation of His word. **Meditation**, as a believer, is the process of the mind thinking, memorizing, and constantly being receptive to revelation from the *"Rhema"* Word of God and the *"Logos"* Word of God. It entails the believer thinking through thoroughly the word of God, whether it be spoken or written. The purpose of meditation involves understanding the word of God, knowing what it means, and gaining knowledge of how that specific word is applicable to our lives. When we have truly accomplished the fullness of meditating on a specific word of God, we are able to interpret the revelation of that word and use it to exercise God's will in our lives.

PSYCHOLOGICAL WARFARE:
Destroying the Power of Negative Words & Negative Thinking

While no longer being believers with a worldly carnal mind, but actually, we become believers transformed and renewed with a spiritual mind; so we can prove what is good, acceptable, and the perfect, will of God.

Romans 12:1-2

I beseech you therefore, brethren, by the mercies of Go, that ye present your bodies a living sacrifice, holy, acceptable unto God, *which is* your reasonable service. And be not conformed to this world: but be ye transformed by the renewing of your mind, that ye may prove what is that good, and acceptable, and perfect, will of God.

Joshua 1:8

This book of the law shall not depart out of thy mouth; but thou shalt meditate therein day and night, that thou mayest observe to do according to all that is written therein: for then thou shalt make thy way prosperous, and
then thou shalt have good success.

I Timothy 4:15

Meditate upon these things; give thyself wholly to them; that thy profiting may appear to all.

In conclusion, it is imperative for us to judge our thinking according to the Word of God. We need to

PSYCHOLOGICAL WARFARE:
Destroying the Power of Negative Words & Negative Thinking

have right thinking, positive thinking, godly thinking with the right mind. We discussed the importance of thinking right thoughts and the value of experiencing the mind renewal process, in order to truly maintain a positive mindset. We also discussed the mind of Christ and how it affects our mental position as believers in the Kingdom of God. We learned that the mind of Christ entails a mind of humility. It is essential that we acknowledge God and surrender to the will of God, because the bible tells us according to, **Matthew 6:24,** No man can serve two masters, for either he will hate the one, and love the other. God has given every man the power of choice. We are free moral agents in the earth realm. We have the right to choose our eternal destiny, as well as, what we should do only a daily basis, this includes our thought life. As you can see our thought life can determine our attitude, character, and behavior. Now, it is time for us to investigate your own thinking. We must continuously confront the thoughts in our mind which opposes the word of God. There is a mandate for us to live and function with a sound mind. No more

PSYCHOLOGICAL WARFARE:
Destroying the Power of Negative Words & Negative Thinking

negative thoughts, we can not walk in a carnal state of thinking, while trying to live and function with a spiritual mind in the Kingdom of God. Remember, we can transform our negative thoughts into positive thoughts.

Matthew 6:24

No man can serve two masters: for either he will hate the one, and love the other; or else he will hold to the one, and despise the other. Ye cannot serve God and mammon.

PSYCHOLOGICAL WARFARE:
Destroying the Power of Negative Words & Negative Thinking

Identifying Negative Thinking:

Can you identify with the statements below?
_____

Check the statements that you have spoken or thought of in the corridors of your mind:

__They hate me
__I hate them
__They don't like me
__They don't understand me
__No body understand me
__Nobody loves me
__I've been misunderstood all my life
__Life ain't nothing
__I can't do it
__I don't have enough money
__You don't love me
__I don't care if they go to hell
__Do you, cause I'm gonna do me
__they don't treat me right
__If it ain't one thing it's another
__It's always something
__I don't want anyone touching me
__You can't do that
__Y'all don't understand
__Nobody cares about me
__I give up
__When it rains, it pours
__I don't want to be bother
__Move, don't touch me
__When will I be happy

__You can't trust nobody
__I'll never love anyone else
__Everybody is jealous of me
__I don't have enough time
__I'm afraid
__I'm lonely
__I don't want to live
__I don't feel saved
__Nothing working for me
__Am I cursed
__I am not waiting anymore
__I'm tired of being alone
__I don't feel worthy
__Did you forget about me
__I'm tired of waiting
__I don't trust nobody
__People are fake
__What's the point of living
__Forget it, I got it
__I don't feel worthy
__I quit
__I am tired of working
__Leave me alone
__I feel hopeless
__She looks pitiful

Copyright © DR. CHARISSEE LEWIS, 2017

PSYCHOLOGICAL WARFARE:
Destroying the Power of Negative Words & Negative Thinking

__ You are always broke
__ He never tells the truth
__ You never have any money
__ Why are you here
__ Why were you born
__ You have no value
__ Get out, you have no value
__ She thinks she looks good
__ He is so ugly
__ I gave up on people
__ Leave me alone; before I bust you in the mouth
__ Why should I talk; no one is listening
__ Shut up, you are talking too much
__ I thought you said God was blessing you
__ You are never going to finish that project
__ God did you forget about me
__ These kids are getting on my nerves
__ How are you going to do that without money
__ I knew something bad was going happen
__ I did this before, and I'm not doing it again
__ If I want something done, I'll have to do it myself
__ I don't like them, because they don't like me
__ You don't care about me, and I don't care about you
__ I can never get help when I need it
__ If I want something done, I have to do it myself
__ Y'all ..... are getting on my nerves
__ Y'all are getting on my reserve nerves
__ My life is miserable
__ Trust and believe, I will do it if I want too....
__ You can't tell me what to do
__ Stop questioning me
__ I'm leaving and I am never coming back
__ I will never call you again, you're are dead

Copyright © DR. CHARISSEE LEWIS, 2017

PSYCHOLOGICAL WARFARE:
Destroying the Power of Negative Words & Negative Thinking

Changing Negative Thoughts into Positive Thoughts

- Take out eight statements you chose, and find a scripture that refute the negative thought pattern, and turn the negative thought into a positive thought and statement.

For example:

<u>**Negative**</u>
- I can't do it

<u>**Positive**</u>
Philippians 4:13
I can do all things through Christ which strengthens me.

1. _____ _____

2. _____ _____

3. _____ _____

4. _____ _____

5. _____ _____

6. _____ _____

7. _____ _____

8. _____ _____

PSYCHOLOGICAL WARFARE:
Destroying the Power of Negative Words & Negative Thinking

CONDITIONS OF THE MIND:

- The conditions of the mind entails the disposition, character, and the state of health of the mind. It also involves identifying anything that modifies, and restricts the nature of the mind.

- Check off the conditions which apply to your mind.

( ) A Mind of Affliction
( ) Analytical Mind
( ) Anxious Mind
( ) A Mind of Giving
( ) Anointed Mind
( ) A Beautiful Mind
( ) A Mind of Business
( ) Carnal Mind
( ) A Mind of Christ
( ) A Mind of Compromise
( ) Confident Mind
( ) Confused Mind
( ) Controlling Mind
( ) Creative Mind
( ) Critical Mind
( ) A Mind of Corruption
( ) Demonic Mind
( ) Depressed Mind
( ) Distrustful Mind
( ) Dominate Mind

( ) Fearful Mind
( ) Forgetful Mind
( ) Focused Mind
( ) Ghetto Mind
( ) Gifted Mind
( ) Grateful Mind
( ) Hopeful Mind
( ) Humble Mind
( ) Impatient Mind
( ) Intelligent Mind
( ) Judgmental Mind
( ) Negative Mind
( ) Passive Mind
( ) Patient Mind
( ) Peaceful Mind
( ) Perverted Mind
( ) A Mind of Praise
( ) Prayerful Mind
( ) Prideful Mind
( ) Prophetic Mind

PSYCHOLOGICAL WARFARE:
Destroying the Power of Negative Words & Negative Thinking

CONDITIONS OF THE MIND: (con't)

( ) Doubtful Mind
( ) A Mind of Ego
( ) Evil Mind
( ) A Mind of Excellence
( ) Extraordinary Mind
( ) Schizophrenic Mind
( ) Selfish Mind
( ) Spiritual Mind
( ) Supernatural Mind
( ) A Mind of Confusion
( ) Suspicious Mind
( ) Stubborn Mind
( ) Unbelieving Mind
( ) Unforgiving Mind
( ) A Mind of Uncertainty
( ) A Mind of Vision
( ) Vindictive Mind
( ) A Positive Mind
( ) A Confrontational Mind
( ) Emotional Mind
( ) Crooked Mind
( ) An Honest Mind
( ) A Mind of Truth
( ) A Mind of Purpose
( ) Receptive Mind
( ) A Mind of Justice

( ) Prosperous Mind
( ) Rebellious Mind
( ) Revengeful Mind
( ) A Mind of Revelation
( ) Scattered Mind
( ) Wandering Mind
( ) A Mind of Manipulation
( ) Wicked Mind
( ) Worried Mind
( ) A Mind of Reasoning
( ) A Mind of Worship
( ) Wondering Mind
( ) A Mind of Divination
( ) An Occultic Mind
( ) A Mind of Sorcery
( ) A Barbarous Mind
( ) A Mind of Witchcraft
( ) Opened Mind
( ) Unstable Mind
( ) A Naïve Mind
( ) Twisted Mind
( ) A Mind of Faith
( ) An Hindering Mind
( ) Broad-Minded
( ) Teachable Mind
( ) Temperamental Mind

Copyright © DR. CHARISSEE LEWIS, 2017

PSYCHOLOGICAL WARFARE:
Destroying the Power of Negative Words & Negative Thinking

CONDITIONS OF THE MIND: (con't)

- ( ) A Slothful Mind
- ( ) A Mind of Procrastination
- ( ) Tormented Mind
- ( ) Loving Mind
- ( ) A Strong Mind
- ( ) A Deceptive Mind
- ( ) A Trustworthy Mind
- ( ) A Triumph Mind
- ( ) A Mind of Servitude
- ( ) A Mind of Warfare
- ( ) A Bombarded Mind
- ( ) An Oppressed Mind
- ( ) A Mind of Wisdom
- ( ) An Adventurous Mind
- ( ) An Abusive Mind
- ( ) An Active Mind
- ( ) A Delusional Mind
- ( ) A Mind of Mockery
- ( ) A Historical Mind
- ( ) A Mind of Diligence
- ( ) A Mind of a Champion

- ( ) Jealous Mind
- ( ) Covetous Mind
- ( ) Passive Mind
- ( ) Angry Mind
- ( ) A Stubborn Mind
- ( ) A Mind of Truth
- ( ) Aggressive Mind
- ( ) Victorious Mind
- ( ) A Mind of Grace
- ( ) Visionary Mind
- ( ) A Overwhelmed Mind
- ( ) A Delusional Mind
- ( ) A Disciplined Mind
- ( ) A Mind of Compassion
- ( ) A Creative Mind
- ( ) A Fortified Mind
- ( ) A Mind of Certainty
- ( ) A Mind of Intellect
- ( ) A Gifted Mind
- ( ) A Mind of Resources
- ( ) Overworked Mind

PSYCHOLOGICAL WARFARE:
Destroying the Power of Negative Words & Negative Thinking

Now that you have examined yourself and honestly checked off the *Conditions of the Mind*, you are ready to move forward to complete the assignment. I want you to list the number of **negative conditions** you checked off; and list the number of **positive conditions** you checked off.

NEGATIVE MIND CONDITIONS:
_____
_____
_____
_____
_____
_____
_____
_____

POSITIVE MIND CONDITIONS:
_____
_____
_____
_____
_____
_____
_____
_____

Now that you have identified your **negative mind conditions**, it is time for to *renounce* the negative mind conditions and pray for a new paradigm and healing in your mind!

PSYCHOLOGICAL WARFARE:
Destroying the Power of Negative Words & Negative Thinking

Prayer for the Conditions of the Mind

Father in the Name of Jesus Christ, I come to You with a repentance heart, seeking Your face for forgiveness. Today, I realize that I am dealing with battles in my mind and I want to change my mentality, in Jesus' Name. Lord, I want to have a healthy mental view of life and those around me, in Jesus' Name. Lord Jesus, please change the conditions of my mind and my disposition, my character, and the state of health of my mind, in Jesus' Name. In time pasts, the conditions of mind have been evil, full of negativity, and even confused; but now, I want to be healed in my mind and free from oppressing thoughts, in Jesus' Name. I rebuke, refute, and dismantle every negative condition that is infiltrating my mind, in Jesus' Name. I call out these negative conditions right now: this includes an angry mind, a barbarous mind, a confused mind, a controlling mind, a critical mind, a mind of corruption, a crooked mind, a deceptive mind, a demonic mind, a depressed mind, a distrustful mind, a mind of divination, a dominate

PSYCHOLOGICAL WARFARE:
Destroying the Power of Negative Words & Negative Thinking

Prayer for the Conditions of the Mind
(con't)

mind, a doubtful mind, an evil mind, a fearful mind, a ghetto mind, an impatient mind, a jealous mind, a judgmental mind, a passive mind, a perverted mind, a prideful mind, a mind of procrastination, a rebellious mind, a revengeful mind, a scattered mind, a schizophrenic mind, a selfish mind, a slothful mind, a mind of sorcery, a suspicious mind, a stubborn mind, a tormented mind, a twisted mind, an unbelieving mind, an unforgiving mind, an unstable mind, a vindictive mind, a wicked mind, a mind of witchcraft, and a worried mind, in Jesus' Name. I loose an healthy mind, an anointed mind, a beautiful mind, a mind of business, the mind of Christ, a confident mind, a creative mind, a mind of excellence, an extraordinary mind, a focused mind, a gifted mind, a mind of grace, a grateful mind, an holy mind, an hopeful mind, a humble mind, an intelligent mind, a loving mind, a patient mind, a peaceful mind, a mind of praise, a prayerful mind, a prophetic mind, a mind

PSYCHOLOGICAL WARFARE:
Destroying the Power of Negative Words & Negative Thinking

Prayer for the Conditions of the Mind
(con't)

of positivity, a prosperous mind, a mind of revelation, a spiritual mind, a mind of worship, a strong mind, a supernatural mind, a triumph mind, a trustworthy mind, a mind of worship, and a mind of vision, in Jesus' Name. Thank You, Father for renewing the conditions of my mind and healing me from old thoughts patterns, and old paradigms, in Jesus' Name. I thank You, Father God, for healing my mind from negative thought patterns, in Jesus' Name. I welcome new innovative ideals which will increase me and cause me to grow spiritually, mentally, emotionally, academically, and financially, in Jesus' Name. I also welcome new revelations, dreams, and visions concerning my position in the Kingdom of God, in Jesus' Name. Thank You, Father God in the mighty name of Jesus Christ! Amen!

PSYCHOLOGICAL WARFARE:
Destroying the Power of Negative Words & Negative Thinking

Chapter Six

EXPOSING WICKED IMAGINATIONS

Have you ever felt strongly about a person or situation, only to discover your thoughts concerning the person or situation were totally wrong? Have you ever imagined something bad about a person, and found out what you thought about the person was the total opposite of the truth? Have you ever been falsely accused of doing something? Yet, no matter how you tried to defend yourself; the person whom accused you still thought you were guilty? The imagination of man is a powerful tool God has given mankind to create, invent, and to see into the future; especially when we tap into the prophetic mind of our Sovereign God. Unfortunately, many people's mind and imagination are *distorted* and *defiled* by the spirits of perversion and delusions; which causes the mind and imagination to be altered, entrapped, bound by illusions, and evil spirits. Numerous believers of today's generation have lost their ability to create and

PSYCHOLOGICAL WARFARE:
Destroying the Power of Negative Words & Negative Thinking

think positively; because their souls are oppressed by invading thoughts of negativity, perversion, deception, and wickedness.

In this chapter, we will expose how a wicked imagination affects the heart, mind, behavior, and belief system of a person. We will expose the mentality of a person whose imagination is damaged, defiled, and infiltrated by deception, perversion, and insecurities. Let's begin by examining the scripture in the Book of Titus,

Titus 1:15

Unto the pure all things are pure: but unto them that are defiled and unbelieving is nothing pure; but even their mind and conscience is defiled.

The word **"pure"** means to be free from all kinds of contamination. This scripture informs us when a person has a pure mind, and a pure heart, then he can see and perceive in depth; the purity in others. However, when a person's mind is defiled and unbelieving it is dirty, unclean, and deceived by the

PSYCHOLOGICAL WARFARE:
Destroying the Power of Negative Words & Negative Thinking

lies of the enemy. A defiled imagination can become a haven for false wicked thoughts, a wicked imagination, and evil actions. A person with a wicked imagination can become very dangerous; if he believes untruths and falsehoods that are perceived from his sensory realm, and past experiences. It is sad to see, numerous relationships being destroyed because of wicked imaginations, negative thoughts, and wrong perceptions. There are too many believers victimized and falsely accused by others Christians who feel they are using the gift of discerning of spirits; when truly, they are operating out of a defiled imagination and while speaking lies perceived through a perverse imagination. A defiled imagination can incite greater insecurities and distrust to a person who is already dealing with feelings of insecurity, inadequacies, and jealousy. The devil takes advantage of an insecure person's imagination by showing him visions that are not true about the people he loves. Then the devil continues to oppress that person by adding evil thoughts to support the false visions in the wicked imagination of that person, be it Christian or

PSYCHOLOGICAL WARFARE:
Destroying the Power of Negative Words & Negative Thinking

Non-Christian. When a person's mind and imagination is defiled they will think evil thoughts that are conjured up out of the realm of darkness. Until this person is healed and delivered in their soul, from past hurts and the memories of negative experiences: his mind will continue to be infiltrated and influenced by negativity while hindering his ability to see positively and perceive in purity. He will continue to function with a wicked imagination; not trusting others and believing every lie the enemy suggests about other people. The bible discusses evil thoughts and evil imagination in the scriptures. Let's examine God's view on this important subject.

Psalm 94:11

The Lord knoweth the thoughts of man, that they *are* vanity.

Proverbs 15:26

The thoughts of the wicked *are* an abomination to the Lord: but *the words* of the pure are pleasant words.

PSYCHOLOGICAL WARFARE:
Destroying the Power of Negative Words & Negative Thinking

Proverbs 23:7

For as he thinketh in his heart, so *is* he: Eat and drink, saith he to thee; but his heart *is* not with thee.

Proverbs 24:9

The thought of foolishness is sin: and the scorner is an abomination to men.

Matthew 9:4

And Jesus knowing their thoughts said, Wherefore think ye evil in your hearts?

Psalm 38:12

They also that seek after my life lay snares for me: and they that seek my hurt speak mischievous things, and imagine deceits all the day long.

Ezekiel 8:12

Then said he unto me, Son of man, hast thou seen what the ancients of the house of Israel do in the dark, every man in the chambers of his imagery? For they say, The Lord seeth us not; the Lord hath forsaken the earth.

PSYCHOLOGICAL WARFARE:
Destroying the Power of Negative Words & Negative Thinking

Romans 1:21

Because that, when they knew God, they glorified him not as God, neither were thankful; but became vain in their imaginations, and their foolish heart was darkened.

In studying the scriptures on this page and the previous page, it is revealed to us that the Lord knows the thoughts of man, consist of vanity. The word **"vanity"** means to be self-absorbed with our appearance, our possessions, and our achievements. The scriptures also indicate to us the thoughts of the wicked are an abomination to the Lord. The word **"abomination"** is defined as extreme disgust, so the scriptures are telling us the thoughts of the wicked are extremely disgusting to our God. With that being said, this is why it is so important for us to think good thoughts and to speak pure words. When a person is thinking evil and wickedly, eventually he will say wicked words, and behave in an evil way. These are just a few explanations concerning God's view on the thoughts of the wicked. Now, let's discuss what the scriptures are saying about an evil imagination.

PSYCHOLOGICAL WARFARE:
Destroying the Power of Negative Words & Negative Thinking

In **Psalm 38:12**, the scripture talks about those who seek to lay snares are people who speak mischievous words and imagine deceits all day long. Unfortunately, there are people who try to lay snares, schemes, and traps to destroy the success of others, and they speak words intending to cause harm to the people they are targeting. The bible says they imagine deceits, artfully create ways of slyness, and misrepresentation of the truth. Often times, these kinds of people practice deception, evil, and wickedness against innocent people. These people are morally wrong with corrupt imaginations and they practice falsehoods and untruths. Sometimes, people with wicked imaginations are spiritually gifted and are able to receive revelation from God, and the devil. The problem is, they too are deceived by the enemy and become victims who believe the false revelation, in which they see. The devil is the father of lies and there is no truth in him. He is a master of deception and he can use the imagination of man to show false images and visions of untruths, to ignite a ball of confusion. Confusion comes when a spiritually gifted

PSYCHOLOGICAL WARFARE:
Destroying the Power of Negative Words & Negative Thinking

person thinks what he sees or perceives is from the realm and knowledge of God; but really, it is from the realm of satan operating through the soul of man. This kind of mentality can become very tormenting to a person who is spiritually gifted but do not know how to operate the spiritual gifts, in alignment with the Holy Spirit. As a result, they perceive through their senses (flesh) and an unclean imagination. This is a clear reason why believers should read the word of God so we can know the difference between the spirit and the soul. This also why our thoughts and imagination need to be pure and honest. The scripture in Philippians tells us we should live and think with these virtues.

Philippians 4:8

Finally, brethren, whatsoever things are <u>true</u>, whatsoever things *are* <u>honest</u>, whatsoever things *are* <u>just</u>, whatsoever things *are* <u>pure</u>, whatsoever things *are* <u>lovely</u>, whatsoever things *are* of <u>good report</u>; if *there be* <u>any</u> <u>virtue</u>, and if *there be* <u>any praise</u>, think on these things.

PSYCHOLOGICAL WARFARE:
Destroying the Power of Negative Words & Negative Thinking

The devil is constantly looking for carnal minds and hostile minds, in which he can use to hurt those who are living in purity. It so unfair for a person with a healthy mind and a healthy imagination: to be in a relationship, friendship, partnership, or marriage with a person who has a defiling imagination. People with defiled imaginations can destroy relationships, marriages, jobs, businesses and churches, because they can falsely accuse innocent people based upon false visions, false dreams, and false revelation; they have envisioned through their own imagination and sometimes through the defiling imagination of others. It is imperative for prophets, intercessors, and believers to allow the Holy Spirit to cleanse our soul from the hurts and sins of our past. We cannot allow satan to infiltrate our heart, mind, and our imagination with wicked thoughts and defiling visions. We must allow the Spirit of God to cleanse our thoughts and our imagination from the oppression of satan. Satan wants to bombard our mind with a system of deception to make us unwilling to trust others. His aim is to infiltrate, intimidate,

PSYCHOLOGICAL WARFARE:
Destroying the Power of Negative Words & Negative Thinking

frustrate, isolate, and dominate our mind, so he can control our thoughts, our imagination, and our behavior. The bible says, in **Proverbs 23:7**, *for as a man thinketh in his heart, so is he.* The heart represents the spirit of man; this is the hidden man which cannot be seen with the natural eyes. The thoughts in our heart reveal the true essence of who we are; because these thoughts are from our spiritual man. This is why it is crucial for believers to acknowledge we have a spirit, and a soul. Our spirit gives us access to commune with God and to receive truth from God. In understanding this knowledge, we will be able to identify true thoughts that are derived from our spirit and false thoughts that come from our defiled imagination.

In conclusion, we must identify thoughts and visions that are not from God. Many people have lost loving relationships and friendships, because their mind and imagination is defiled and wicked. We cannot allow pride and fear to stop us from confronting the evil thoughts that may lurk in our

PSYCHOLOGICAL WARFARE:
Destroying the Power of Negative Words & Negative Thinking

imagination. The devil ultimately wants to damage and destroy the spirit of man, and contaminate and corrupt the soul. He wants human race to be deceived, eternally damned, and sentenced to the lake of fire. It is essential for us to understand the function of the spirit and the soul, so we can protect ourselves from the attacks of satan. Through the knowledge of God, we can be free from the oppression and torment of satan!

Now, we will look introspectively at man; and discuss specifically the function and operation of the **spirit** and the **soul**.

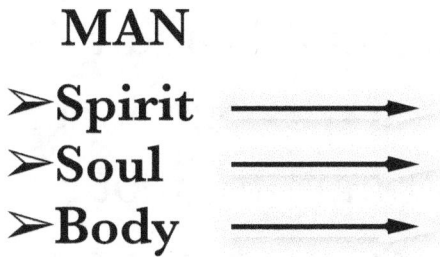

1. Conscience, Intuition, and Communion.
2. Mind, Will, Emotion, Imagination, Memory, and Intellect.
3. Flesh, Senses, Blood, Sinew, Bones,

PSYCHOLOGICAL WARFARE:
Destroying the Power of Negative Words & Negative Thinking

THE FUNCTION AND OPERATION OF THE SPIRIT & SOUL

God made man a triune being: we are spirit beings, with a soul, and we live in a human body. The **spirit** of man is hidden to the natural eye. It is called our *spiritual* man; which entails our **conscience, intuition,** and **communion.** The conscience of man gives us the ability to detect and discern what is good and bad, and what is right and wrong. The conscience of man is not influenced or affected by any outside influences or previous knowledge in the subconscious. Our intuition gives us the ability to sense within our human spirit. It gives the inward knowing with a direct answer with confidence. Our intuition is not affected by our emotions which exist in our soulish realm. Next, is communion and this is the organ of worship within our spirit, our inner man. When we worship God, it is straight from our human spirit, not within the soulish realm of our emotions. Pure worship comes from our spiritual man, which has to be acknowledged through submission to God. Through our spiritual man we have access to

PSYCHOLOGICAL WARFARE:
Destroying the Power of Negative Words & Negative Thinking

commune with our Lord & Savior Jesus Christ. It is through our spirit man we can talk to God, and receive revelation of truth that comes directly from Him into our spirit!

Secondly, man has a soul. The **soul** part of man consists of our **mind, will, emotions, imagination, memory,** and **intellect.** Through the soul, man is able to feel, think, make choices, memorize, and learn. The mind is an organ of thought; this is where man think. The will is the organ of choice and desire. The emotion is an organ of feelings. This is where we chose to be happy or sad. In the emotions, we display our mental reactions to issues, problems, or life. The imagination is the organ in the soul, will allows us to create, form new ideals, and see things that are not present in the physical realm. The memory of man is the organ in the soul which remembers and stores information. Lastly, intellect is the organ of knowledge. All of these organs functions in the soul of humanity. It is imperative for us to understand each function, so we can recognize and identify

PSYCHOLOGICAL WARFARE:
Destroying the Power of Negative Words & Negative Thinking

when our soul needs to be healed, cleansed, delivered, and saved from the demonic oppression and onslaughts of satan. We must be able to recognize when we are not functioning appropriately in our spirit and our soul. Understanding the function of the spirit and the soul, gives us knowledge to address specific areas that need healing and development.

Thirdly, the **natural** of part of man entails the physical body which consists of **flesh, senses, blood, bones, organs, sinew** and any other element which makes up the human body. So you can see we are triune being: Spirit, Soul, and Body. Liken unto the Godhead: God the Father, God the Son, God the Holy Spirit. God created man in His own image and likeness. Every part of mankind has a unique function in the design of man.

In summary, we have exposed wicked imaginations, and how it affects our ability to

PSYCHOLOGICAL WARFARE:
Destroying the Power of Negative Words & Negative Thinking

perceive, receive, and understand truth. God created us to use our imagination to invent, create, and move into new dimensions of revelation in the spiritual realm. As stated previously, the imagination exists in the soul of man. It is considered the faculty of imagining, allowing the mind to form new ideas, sensations, and images of creativity. If we did not use all the faculties of our soul, we would be like robots. Reader, remember we are human and divine! The divinity of man is the nature of God on the inside of us. It is our spirit man, which gives us direct contact to commune with our God. Within our soul, God wants us to be renewed in the spirit of our mind; so we can have the mind of Christ, a spiritual mind and think good thoughts. God created our imagination for the betterment of humanity. However, when it is defiled, distorted, and deceived; it can be use by satan to bring detriment to humanity. It is crucial for us (believers) to worship, pray, and renew our minds daily with the word of God. Communing with the Lord daily will assist believers in cleansing our heart, mind, and imagination from the old paradigms of our

PSYCHOLOGICAL WARFARE:
Destroying the Power of Negative Words & Negative Thinking

past. The strongholds lying dormant in the corridors of the heart and soul of man has been exposed in this chapter. Therefore, it is time for us to destroy all evil thoughts and the wickedness contaminating our imagination. Please study the diagram below.

SPIRIT

SOUL **BODY**

MAN
TRIUNE BEING

PSYCHOLOGICAL WARFARE:
Destroying the Power of Negative Words & Negative Thinking

ATTRIBUTES and SINS OF THE WICKED

ASSIGNMENT: Read Psalm Chapter 10 and study the attributes and sins of the wicked below and on the next few pages; then answer the questions following.

1} The wicked is full of pride. {v. 2, 4} Pride causes the wicked to judge and talk about others. It also causes the wicked to be unteachable and detached from the people of God.

2} The wicked persecutes the poor. {v. 2} They talk about those who are weak and harass them persistently. They belittle those who they feel who lives in lack.

3} The wicked sets snares and devices for the just. {v. 2} They create tricks, traps, schemes, and plots with an aim to discredit, and destroy the integrity of the just.

4} The wicked imagines evil against righteous. {v. 2} They think and envision bad and evil activity against righteous folks.

5} The wicked boasts of his great plans. {v. 3} They broadcast and brag of what they want to do for themselves. They talk about themselves regularly.

PSYCHOLOGICAL WARFARE:
Destroying the Power of Negative Words & Negative Thinking

ATTRIBUTES and SINS OF THE WICKED (con't)

6} The wicked blesses the covetous. {v. 3} The wicked come into agreement and alliance those who are materialistic and greedy. They also give to those who have strong desire for someone else's possessions.

7} The wicked rejects and refuses to seek God. {v. 4} They do not think about God nor do they obey His word.

8} The wicked travails to bring forth. {v. 5} The bible says his ways are grievous which means whatever he does it is hard and of a very bad nature. This is a terrible way to live.

9} The wicked disregards and dismisses religion. {v. 5} He refuses to acknowledge the word of God and to develop a personal relationship with God.

10} The wicked is blind to God's judgments. {v. 5} When they are engaging in evil activity they ignore the fact that God is omniscient; He is all seeing and judging everything they do.

11} The wicked puffs at his enemies. {v. 5} This scripture indicates the wicked talk a lot about their enemies, but never really confront an issue with their enemies.

PSYCHOLOGICAL WARFARE:
Destroying the Power of Negative Words & Negative Thinking

ATTRIBUTES and SINS OF THE WICKED (con't)

12} The wicked boasts of getting what he wants {v. 6} The wicked is full of so much pride and self-gratification; he purposes in his heart he will not be distracted nor stopped from receiving what he wants. He is not concerned about adversity.

13} The wicked blasphemes {v. 7} This scripture says the mouth of the wicked is full of cursing (foul language), deceit, and fraud. This tells of the mouth of the wicked is dishonest, negative, and fake. You cannot believe what comes out of his mouth, because he is fake and intends to deceive.

14} The wicked deceives others {v. 7} The wicked mislead and beguile others for self-gain. They cause others to have wrong ideas or impressions about someone or something.

15} The wicked cheats others {v. 7} The scripture says the mouth of the wicked is full of cursing, deceit, and fraud; this means the words of the wicked are intended to express evil, hurt, and deception to others.

PSYCHOLOGICAL WARFARE:
Destroying the Power of Negative Words & Negative Thinking

ATTRIBUTES and SINS OF THE WICKED (con't)

16} The wicked speaks mischief and vanity {v. 7} This scripture also says under their tongue is mischief and vanity. Therefore, the foundation of what the wicked speaks derives from a spirit of pride to incite trouble and disobedience.

17} The wicked plots against neighbors {v. 8} This scripture says the wicked sits in lurking places; meaning they sit in places that are hidden so they can ambush others.

18} The wicked murders the innocent {v. 8} The wicked plot in secret places to murder the weak ones. A murderer is a person who kill unlawfully and with premeditation, literally and with their tongues.

19} The wicked takes advantage of the weak {v. 8} The wicked eyes are secretly set to hurt the poor. The wicked bullies those they feel are weak and insignificant.

20} The wicked plots against the poor {v. 9} In this passage, the wicked is symbolized as a lion watching for its prey. Then as a hunter taking wild animals into his net and then as a wild beast crushing his prey.

PSYCHOLOGICAL WARFARE:
Destroying the Power of Negative Words & Negative Thinking

ATTRIBUTES and SINS OF THE WICKED (con't)

21} The wicked manifests cruelty. {v. 10} The wicked take pleasure in causing pain, suffering, and callous indifference. This scripture says he acts harmless through False humility only to cause the poor to fall prey to his wicked friends. Also in the symbolism of an lion, the poor would be destroyed by his claws and powerful teeth.

22} The wicked lives secure in his sins {v. 11} This scripture is revealing the false security of the wicked. It shows the process of how satan has deceived the wicked in his heart. He thinks God is not going to remember his evil doings. Sadly, he is also deceived to think God is not concerned enough about him to see his evil activities.

Please Answer the following Questions:

1} Do you identify with any of the characteristics of the wicked? _____.

2} Are there any areas of pride in your life? _____.

3} Do you imagine evil things against the righteous? ____.

4} Do you mistreat the poor? _____.

PSYCHOLOGICAL WARFARE:
Destroying the Power of Negative Words & Negative Thinking

THE SPIRIT of DELUSION & THE IMAGINATION of MAN

There are many demonic spirits that can infiltrate the imagination of man to alter his reality of truth. We discovered the **spirit of delusion** is a deep spirit that affects the soul of an individual. This is a deceiving spirit that is a major symptom and an intricate element in numerous mental disorders, especially other psychotic disorders. It attacks the perception of a person which causes them to persistently believe something as truth, wrongly and mistakenly; in spite of the evidence being contrary to the reality of a situation. The spirit of delusion causes a person to hold as truth a belief, conviction, or altered reality even when there is insurmountable evidence to oppose what a person may be claiming as truth. A person with this spirit will be strong and wrong even though, truth may be factual and apparent. The spirit of delusion works with the mind and the wicked imagination to lay a foundation of deception within the soul of a person, making them

PSYCHOLOGICAL WARFARE:
Destroying the Power of Negative Words & Negative Thinking

a victim of the lies of satan. The spirit of delusion is an intricate part of mental illnesses and mental disorders. It is imperative for us to identify the level of deception that is oppression the mind of an individual. We must be able to discern truth about a person through educational knowledge, revelation knowledge, the gift of discerning of spirits, the word of God, and the Holy Spirit. When it comes to the spirit of delusion it can be layered to hide the disorder a person my be experiencing. This why we find it necessary to expose some of the signs, symptoms, and manifestation of delusional disorders and mental illnesses. Below and on the next few pages, we will inform you and educate you on the behaviors of those who may be oppressed and mentally challenged due to delusional disorders and mental illnesses.

PSYCHOLOGICAL WARFARE:
Destroying the Power of Negative Words & Negative Thinking

Delusional Disorders & Mental Illnesses

- **Delusional Disorder** – It is a mental illness in which the patient sees delusions. A person with delusional disorders may still socialize with others and function in a normal way. His behavior may not be odd, but his thoughts and ideas will be delusional and disruptive to his daily living.

- **Mental Illness** – Mental illness deals a variety of mental health conditions, such as disorders which affects the behavior, mood, and thinking of a person.

- **Alzheimer** – This is a neurodegenerative disease which affects the memory, as it advances it also affects the ability to care for oneself, disorientation, mood swings, loss of motivation, and behavioral issues.

- **Bipolar Disorder** – This is a mental illness and brain disorder, known as manic-depression which causes strange mood shifts. It causes a person to have extreme emotional highs and severe emotional lows and changes in behavior, energy, sleep, and thinking.

- **Capgras Delusion-** A person with this type of delusional disorder believes a love one has been replaced by an imposter, this is delusional misidentification.

- **Dementia** – A person with dementia has a decline in mental abilities such as memory, which affects and interferes with normal living conditions on a daily basis.

PSYCHOLOGICAL WARFARE:
Destroying the Power of Negative Words & Negative Thinking

Delusional Disorders & Mental Illnesses {cont}

- **Erotomanic Delusion** – A person with this type of delusional disorder thinks a famous person is in love with him. Sometimes this person becomes a stalker.

- **Grandiose Delusion** – A person with this type of delusional disorder think he has great powers, knowledge, and identity.

- **Hallucination** – A person with this type of delusional disorder has an experience involving the apparent perception of something not present. It is a sensory experience of something that does not exist outside the mind. It is caused by a reaction to certain toxic substances, and manifested by visual and auditory images.

- **Jealous** - A person with this type of delusional disorder believes that his or her spouse or sexual partner is being unfaithful and cheating.

- **Monothematic Delusion** – A person with this type of delusional disorder concerns only one particular topic. This person has an isolated delusion that is a wrong and mistaken idea that does not have a basis for reality.

- **Paranoid Schizophrenia** – A person with this mental disorder loses touch with reality, and the he will hallucinate, while hearing voices and experience delusions.

Copyright © DR. CHARISSEE LEWIS, 2017

PSYCHOLOGICAL WARFARE:
Destroying the Power of Negative Words & Negative Thinking

Delusional Disorders & Mental Illnesses {cont}

A person with this mental illness may sometime be disorganized in speech and conversations.

- **Persecutory Delusion** – A person with this type of delusional disorder thinks he is being followed and someone is trying to harm him.

- **Polythematic Delusions** – A person with this type of has a range of delusions: such as schizophrenia or dementia or they can occur without any other signs of mental illness. When this type of disorder can also occur through neurological illness, strokes, and traumatic brain injuries.

- **Psychosis** – A person with this kind of disorder has an abnormal condition of the mind which involves a loss of contact with reality. This person may display personality changes, thought disorders, bizarre or unusual behavior, difficulty with social interaction and day to day living.

- **Religious Delusion** – A person with this type of delusional disorder are focused on religious subjects that are not in alignment with the belief.

- **Somatic Delusion** – A person with this type of delusional disorder believes that he has a physical defect.

PSYCHOLOGICAL WARFARE:
Destroying the Power of Negative Words & Negative Thinking

It is necessary for us to determine the mental state of those who are in our atmosphere. We must recognize when we being attacked in our mind. Also, we must discern and identify those around us who may be dealing with wicked imaginations, evil thoughts, mental illnesses, and/or delusional disorders. When a person's mind is altered by any of these delusional disorders or mental illnesses; spiritual, mental, and professional help is needed to assist in the healing plan of that individual's mind. The questions provided is to make you aware of your emotions and if necessary we encourage you to receive the help you need to maintain a healthy mind.

ASSIGNMENT: Please answer the following questions.

1. Do you suffer with feelings of anxiety?_____

2. If yes, how frequent and when? _____

3. Do have you irregular sleeping patterns?_____

4. If yes, do you suffer with insomnia? _____

Copyright © DR. CHARISSEE LEWIS, 2017

PSYCHOLOGICAL WARFARE:
Destroying the Power of Negative Words & Negative Thinking

5. Do suffer with extended sleeping hours? _____

6. Are you jealous of your spouse? _____

7. Do you feel your spouse is cheating on you? _____

8. Are you depressed? _____

9. Do you have difficulty concentrating? _____

10. Are you suspicious? _____

11. Do you hear voices? _____

12. Do you accuse others of what you saw in your spirit and they constantly deny what you say as truth? _____

13. Are you extremely happy at times and then become severely sad? _____

14. Do you hallucinate? _____

15. Do you have suicidal thoughts and/suicidal actions? _____

16. Do you have disorganized speech and switch topics erratically? _____

Copyright © DR. CHARISSEE LEWIS, 2017

PSYCHOLOGICAL WARFARE:
Destroying the Power of Negative Words & Negative Thinking

In conclusion, it is our prayer that you completed the questions on the previous page. Reader, if you answered yes to at least 3 questions on the previous page; we recommend that you seek professional spiritual counsel so you can be cleansed and healed from all unnatural thoughts, negative, and delusional thinking. We also recommend psychological professional help with a therapist, if you or your love ones are experiencing any of the delusional disorders we shared on pages 152-156. If the delusional disorders or mental illness are interrupting your relationships with others and your daily routine of life; do not hesitate to get the counsel you need. Also, do not allow the spirit of pride to stop you from acknowledging what you may be dealing with mentally. It is crucial for us to have a sound mind, the bible confirms this in the book of II Timothy,

II Timothy 1:7

God hath not given us the spirit of fear; but of power, and of love, and of a sound mind.

PSYCHOLOGICAL WARFARE:
Destroying the Power of Negative Words & Negative Thinking

It is good to receive spiritual counsel from your Spiritual Authority; be it Apostle, Prophetess, Pastor, or whomever has been given stewardship over your soul. If your Spiritual Leader does not counsel, contact us we have a team of counselors on staff. Remember, satan's aim is to bring shame and self-condemnation. He wants us to ignore all symptoms of negativity in the mind, so he can continuously inflict mental, emotional, and psychological hurts in the lives of those who are vulnerable and ignorant of his attacks against the soul of humanity. This is one reason why it is important for us, to expose the different tactics satan uses to oppose and oppress a positive pure mind. We are our brother's keeper. Do not ignore the symptoms of delusional disorders and mental illnesses. You can save your life and the lives of others through the knowledge we have shared with you.

PSYCHOLOGICAL WARFARE:
Destroying the Power of Negative Words & Negative Thinking

DESTROYING WICKED IMAGINATIONS PRAYER

Father in the Name of the Lord Jesus Christ, I come to You with a repentance heart, seeking Your forgiveness for all my sins: sins of omission and sins of commission. Father God, I repent for my evil thoughts and my wicked imagination, in Jesus' Name. I admit I am guilty of misjudging others based on past experiences, and false images in my imagination, in Jesus' Name. Father God, there are times I have preconceived notions about other people, only to discover what I thought about them was not true; I repent in Jesus' Name. Lord Jesus, I ask You to deliver me from the evil that lurks in my mind about others, in Jesus' Name. I want to be set free from evil thoughts and a wicked imagination, in Jesus' Name. Lord Jesus, please cleanse me from my secret faults of iniquity, and revenge, in Jesus' Name. I rebuke and destroy every judgmental spirit, the spirit of unforgiveness, and negative thinking, in Jesus' Name.

Copyright © DR. CHARISSEE LEWIS, 2017

PSYCHOLOGICAL WARFARE:
Destroying the Power of Negative Words & Negative Thinking

DESTROYING WICKED IMAGINATIONS
(con't)

I dismantle, and destroy all roots of bitterness, the gall of bitterness, the wormwood of bitterness, in Jesus' Name. Lord Jesus, I bind and rebuke all spirits attacking my mental health, in Jesus' Name. I decree and declare I am free from the spirit of witchcraft, dominance, controlling spirits, abuse, resentment, fears, insecurities, jealousy, lust, anger, rage, murder, strife, passive aggression, aggressive aggression, bad attitude, deceptions, untruths, evil, falsehood, meanness, rage, moodiness, cruelty, low self-esteem, hurt, malice, abusing others, wickedness, sabotaging spirits, hatred, disharmony, contention, debating, disrespect, distrust, mistrust, callousness of heart, lack of trust, inordinate affections, perversions, bad, destructive, harmful, hateful, wrathful, vicious, spiteful, vile, mockery, sarcasm, loathsome, depravity, debased, corrupt, mental instability, delusional, emotional unstable, mental oppression, mind battles, and mental attacks, in Jesus' Name. I loose clarity of

PSYCHOLOGICAL WARFARE:
Destroying the Power of Negative Words & Negative Thinking

DESTROYING WICKED IMAGINATIONS
(con't)

thoughts and purity in my imagination, in Jesus' Name. My mind is pure and peaceful, in Jesus' Name. My vision is clear in the spiritual and natural realm, in Jesus' Name. I am a good person, with a sound mind and a pure heart, in Jesus' Name. Father God, I thank You for the Spirit of Truth which allows me to speak the truth, hear the truth, see the truth, and receive the truth, in Jesus' Name. I will no longer be a victim of satan, used to speak evil of others, in Jesus' Name. I am a believer and not a doubter, and I shall prophesy to the well-being of others, as an instrument of righteousness, in Jesus' Name. I shall think positive, speak positive, live positive, believe positively, and see the positivity in others, in Jesus' Name. I vow to build up, stir up, and cheer up others, in Jesus' Name. I am healthy in my mind, will, emotions, imagination, memory, and intellect in Jesus' Name. Lord Jesus, You have destroyed the wickedness out of my imagination, now I can dream dreams and see visions

PSYCHOLOGICAL WARFARE:
Destroying the Power of Negative Words & Negative Thinking

DESTROYING WICKED IMAGINATIONS
(con't)

of the future without demonic interference, in Jesus' Name. I shall receive new revelation in my situation because the joy of the Lord is my strength, in Jesus' Name. Father God, I give You all the Glory and the honor in the Name of Jesus Christ, Amen!

PSYCHOLOGICAL WARFARE:
Destroying the Power of Negative Words & Negative Thinking

DESTROYING THE SPIRIT OF DELUSION PRAYER

Father in the Name of Jesus Christ, I give You praise on this day! I come to You humbly in my spirit seeking Your forgiveness for allowing negative thinking to bombard and oppress my mind, in Jesus' Name. I repent for allowing negative thoughts to invade my imagination, in Jesus' Name. I am guilty of falsely accusing love ones of doing wrong towards me, in Jesus' Name. Father God, I have evil thoughts and evil dreams about those who profess to love me, and I want and need to stop evil thinking, in Jesus' Name. I want to be free of the spirit of delusion, in Jesus' Name. Lord Jesus, there are times when I hear voices, that bombard my mind, and I want to be delivered and healed, in Jesus' Name. Lord, I know satan is a master at deception, and his aim is to destroy the mind of man; but I will not allow him to destroy my mind. I realize the spirit of delusion can enter the mind and attack the imagination; causing one to see visions that are not from God. I rebuke the

Copyright © DR. CHARISSEE LEWIS, 2017

PSYCHOLOGICAL WARFARE:
Destroying the Power of Negative Words & Negative Thinking

DESTROYING THE SPIRIT OF DELUSION
(con't)

spirit of delusion, deception, illusions, and evil thought patterns, in Jesus' Name. I loose the spirit of truth, purity, healthy thoughts, and love in heart and mind, that I may see others the way God sees them, in spite of what the enemy may bring to my mind, in Jesus' Name. The spirit of delusion will not deceive and attack my mind any more, in Jesus' Name. My mind is pure, my mind is free, and my mind is at peace, in the Mighty Name of Jesus Christ! Amen.

PSYCHOLOGICAL WARFARE:
Destroying the Power of Negative Words & Negative Thinking

Chapter Seven

IDENTIFYING EMOTIONAL ABUSE

New relationships are fascinating, intriguing, and sometimes adventurous. The excitement of being with a new friend, a new mate, or new marriage can bring our emotions to a climax of genuine love. We are creatures who need to give love and receive love. God created mankind as triune beings, meaning we are spirit, soul, and body. The spirit of man is made of conscience, intuition, and communion. The soul of man consists of our mind, will, emotions, imagination, memory, and intellect. The body of man consists of bones, sinew, muscles, organs, and blood. It is imperative for us to understand and identify where satan uses people to attack us; so we can learn how to fight back, and crush every tactic of the enemy.

Our focus in this chapter is the emotions of man. We can see the emotions reside within the soul. The

PSYCHOLOGICAL WARFARE:
Destroying the Power of Negative Words & Negative Thinking

soul is an important aspect of our being. We know this statement to be true, because satan is constantly launching attacks against the souls of humanity. The kingdom of darkness artfully designs strategies to deceive, blind, and destroy the lives of humanity. Satan also uses his agents to give people false hopes, and false perceptions of God, and false perceptions of God's Kingdom. Satan operates on a system of deception, pride, and control to persuade people into making covenants with him. He pursues the souls of men to enlarge hell.

II Corinthians 4:4

In whom the god of this world hath blinded the minds of them which believe not, lest the light of the glorious gospel of Christ, who is the image of God, should shine unto them.

Isaiah 5:14

Therefore hell hath enlarged herself, and opened her mouth without measure: and their glory, and their multitude, and their pomp, and he that rejoiceth, shall decend into it.

It is important for us to have a healthy soul. The soul contains our mind and emotions, and when the mind

PSYCHOLOGICAL WARFARE:
Destroying the Power of Negative Words & Negative Thinking

and emotions are not healthy: we can be victimized, tormented and destroyed by satan. Ultimately, finding ourselves in hell and eternal damnation. Therefore, it is crucial for us to get our soul in divine order and divine alinement with the will of God for our lives.

With that being said, emotional abuse may be easy to identify when you are not a victim of it. We can identify obvious characteristics of like jealousy, manipulation, and control. Unfortunately, for the person who is victimized and bound by relationship to an emotional abuser; he or she may not be able to readily identify the characteristics of emotional abuse. Emotional abuse is willful intentional infliction of pain and suffering through verbal or non-verbal actions to a human being. It is an infliction of distress and a denial of a person's civil rights. This kind of abuse deals with the psyche of man. The emotional abuser will use a plethora of tactics to incite fear, isolation, manipulation, and control to keep the victim in a state of brokenness and under their thumb. The emotional abuser could be a parent, a relative, a

PSYCHOLOGICAL WARFARE:
Destroying the Power of Negative Words & Negative Thinking

caretaker, a friend, a teacher, a tutor, a supervisor, a business partner, a lover, or even a spouse. The emotional abuser is sometimes subtle in their behavior to seduce and bate a person in their world of abuse. Once the emotional abuser has repeatedly abused the person of target, by constantly criticizing, falsely accusing, blaming, name-calling: it will destroy a person's self-esteem. Then the abuser can take full control of dismantling the self-worth of their target of prey. The emotional abuser will not descend in his or her tactics unless there is a divine intervention. The victim may have to leave the relationship or situation of interest. If you are being emotionally abused, you must get help or walk away from that relationship! No one has a right to belittle a person; be it publicly or privately. It is important for you to feel good about you and value who you are; if the person who supposed to love and value you can not give you a healthy loving relationship; then you must speak up and receive professional help.

PSYCHOLOGICAL WARFARE:
Destroying the Power of Negative Words & Negative Thinking

Emotional abusers tear at the self-esteem of a person. They use words to insult and isolate their victims. They use confusion and control to release mental stress, mental anguish while monitoring their victims. They constantly belittle through acts of humiliation such as yelling, hollering, shouting, and mocking a person publicly to bring hurt and shame. They also release a spirit of fear and intimidation through outbursts of anger and rage, treating and talking to you like a child, threatening you, and going through your personal mail, cell phone, or emails. The emotional abuser will talk about you negatively in front others through mockery, jokes, character assassination, sarcasm, and to make you feel your opinion is not valuable. The final result is negativity. These are just a few characteristics of emotional abuse. On the next page, we have categorized some common symptoms and tactics of abuse and we shared some examples, as well.

PSYCHOLOGICAL WARFARE:
Destroying the Power of Negative Words & Negative Thinking

Tactics of Emotional Abuse

A} Accusations and Blaming:

1) False accusations - Falsely accuse you of doing what they are guilty of doing to you.

2) Blaming You - The abuser will blame you for things going wrong in his life.

3) Destroying Your Items - The abuser may break your television or phone and say you made him do it.

4) Flip the Script - The abuser will get angry with you suddenly, and treat you like an enemy.

5) Guilt - The abuser will try to make you guilty for correcting them for mistreating you.

6) Jealousy - The abuser accuse you of cheating and say you are not a good person.

PSYCHOLOGICAL WARFARE:
Destroying the Power of Negative Words & Negative Thinking

Tactics of Emotional Abuse Con't

B} Criticism and Humiliation:

7) **Assassination of Character** - The abuser tells you can't do anything right and repeatedly attack your character.

8) **Belittling through Jokes** - The abuser mocks and ridicule you through jokes which always makes you look and feel incompetent.

9) **Calling you Names** - The abuser call you names and use negative words to demean you. For example *"you're a dummy or you're stupid"*.

10) **Disdainful Behavior** - The abuser shows a lack of respect towards you by devaluing you, by ignoring you, or displaying a negative disposition in your presence.

11) **Insults your Appearance** - The abuser always makes negative comments about your hair, clothes, or shoes. There is no positive affirmations.

PSYCHOLOGICAL WARFARE:
Destroying the Power of Negative Words & Negative Thinking

Tactics of Emotional Abuse
Con't

C} Control and Causing Shame

12) Controlling the Finances: The abuser has all control over the finances and you have to ask for money, and explain why you need it.

13) Belittling Your Imperfections: The abuser excessively points out your your weaknesses, making you feel shame and subservient to him or her.

14) Manipulation through Pity: The abuser controls you by making you feel sorry for him/her and obligated to do what the abuser wants.

15) Outburst of Anger: The abuser uses anger/rage to control the atmosphere and causing you to cater to their needs cause you don't the abuser to get angry.

PSYCHOLOGICAL WARFARE:
Destroying the Power of Negative Words & Negative Thinking

Tactics of Emotional Abuse Con't

D} Emotional Neglect and Social Isolation

17) **Dividing Your Family:** The abuser brings division between you and your family to isolate you and destroy your support system.

18) **Dividing Your Friendships:** The abuser separates you from your friends and those who support and love you; by creating confusion or talking negatively about you and them.

19) **Emotionally Detached:** The abuser is not connected nor concerned about you emotionally which aids in the continual abuse.

20) **Emotional Sabotage:** The abuser acts like he/she wants to hear how you feel but when you share your feelings; the abuser attacks or ignores you.

21) **Withholding Sex:** The abuser refuses to give spouse affection, intimacy, or sex due to anger and control.

PSYCHOLOGICAL WARFARE:
Destroying the Power of Negative Words & Negative Thinking

The tactics of emotional abuse listed will aide you in identifying whether you are a victim of emotional abuse or whether you are an emotional abuser. Remember, an emotional abuser will make it a common factor to destroy your self-esteem and your self-worth. He or she will use psychological witchcraft and psychological games to confuse your thinking and make you feel inadequate, and fearful. The goal of the emotional abuser is to control you and to belittle you to bend your will to meet their every whim. The emotional abuser uses harsh and barbarous words to repeatedly demean the target of their abuse. Living in an emotionally abusive marriage, can produce mental anguish, stress, heartache, depression, and sickness. Not to mention, delaying, and destroying personal goals of a spouse that does not know how to come out of this kind of abuse. Sadly, we also can find this kind of abuse in friendships, and work environments. In friendships, where one person is constantly minimizing and mocking the other person, this is emotional abuse. If

PSYCHOLOGICAL WARFARE:
Destroying the Power of Negative Words & Negative Thinking

you are open and honest about your feelings and your *"so called"* friend, dismiss, or ignore your truth; this to is a form of emotional abuse. A friend is suppose to sharpen the spiritual, moral, and intellectual life of their friends; as iron will sharpen a knife.

Proverbs 27:17

Iron sharpeneth iron; so a man sharpeneth the countenance of his friend.

As stated before, emotional abuse can occur in a work environment, when you have a negative belligerent supervisor calling people out of their names. This too is a form of emotional abuse; just because a person is working on a job does not mean he has to be degraded, disrespected, and dishonored while doing his job.

In summary, reader wherever the emotional abuse is originating, it must be identified and confronted. Where ever the emotional abuse is rooted; it must be uprooted. You do not have to allow anyone to control, bully, and downgrade your emotions. Do not tolerate

PSYCHOLOGICAL WARFARE:
Destroying the Power of Negative Words & Negative Thinking

abuse of any kind from anyone who devalues your self-worth. It is imperative for humanity to be healthy in our emotions. The lack of mental and emotional health is the reason why so many people are public and private failures. Being emotionally healthy can determine our ability to navigate through traumatic seasons in our lives. It is our prayer, that you will confront emotional abuse and any kind of abuse in your life and your entire family bloodline. You can no longer allow your love ones, spouse, friends, associates, children, and supervisors to mistreat you, and depreciate you. You must speak up and stand up for your rights! You do have a right to be happy and live in peace!

PSYCHOLOGICAL WARFARE:
Destroying the Power of Negative Words & Negative Thinking

DESTROYING EMOTIONAL ABUSE

Father in the Name of Jesus, I come to You humbly in my spirit, asking for Your forgiveness from emotional abuse. I repent for allowing others to mistreat me and not speaking up for myself, in Jesus' Name. Father God, today I identify that I have been a victim of abuse. I have been in abusive relationships and I have abused others. Lord Jesus, it is not Your will for us to be abuse emotionally, psychologically, mentally, and verbally; nor abuse others. Father God, You did not create us to hurt, mistreat, or inflict pain on anyone, in Jesus' Name. Lord Jesus, I am asking for healing from emotional abuse, in Jesus Name. Lord Jesus, I need a healing from the trauma of emotional abuse, in Jesus' Name. I desire to be free from the scars of rejection, mental pain, suffering, heartache, disappointment, depression, and discouragement which arise from the hurt of emotional abuse, in Jesus' Name. Lord Jesus, I denounce the witchcraft, control, and shame that makes me feel obligated to stay in a relationship of disrespect and dishonor, in Jesus' Name. I refuse to be

PSYCHOLOGICAL WARFARE:
Destroying the Power of Negative Words & Negative Thinking

DESTROYING EMOTIONAL ABUSE
(Con't)

belittled and minimized any longer, in Jesus' Name. Lord Jesus, help me to increase my self-esteem and my self-worth; so I can move forward in my purpose, in Jesus' Name. I will not ignore the tactics of emotional abuse, in Jesus' Name. I will not live in fear and intimidation any longer, in Jesus' Name. I am strong in the Lord and in the power of His might, in Jesus' Name. I will put on the whole armor of God and crush every negative word than has been spoken to me, in Jesus' Name. Lord Jesus, I know You created me with value and I will no longer sacrifice my love, time, and money to appease the emotional abuser, in Jesus' Name. I will no longer be a victim to the demonic behavior of abuser, in Jesus' Name. I am more than a conqueror, in Jesus' Name. I am an overcomer, in Jesus' Name. Lord Jesus, I shall ascend from this situation and be who You called me to be and I will always identify, confront, and destroy emotional abuse, in the Mighty Name of Jesus, Amen!

PSYCHOLOGICAL WARFARE:
Destroying the Power of Negative Words & Negative Thinking

Chapter Eight

THE SPIRIT OF WITCHCRAFT

The spirit of witchcraft is an evil vile spirit from the dark kingdom used by satanic agents to bind, blind, and bend the will of others. This spirit comes to force a person to do something against the principles and standards of the One and Only True and Living God. The spirit of witchcraft causes its agents to use spirit guides, demons, and satan's co-horts to gain access to control, dominate, frustrate, intimidate, and manipulate others to do what they want. Witches and warlocks use many different things to work their craft; such as astro projection, crystals, burning sage, drinking blood, burying personal items, using pictures, snakes, cats, bats, birds, poisons, charms, and even incantations, which are demonic chants. An incantation is a series of words spoken to invoke a magic spell. Many people do not realize that speaking negative words against the will of God in a person's

PSYCHOLOGICAL WARFARE:
Destroying the Power of Negative Words & Negative Thinking

life is too, witchcraft in operation. It is imperative we bring to your attention, that your negative words, negative opinions, and negative comments repeatedly spoken is all witchcraft. Yes, when you just want to speak your negativity against a person, and you are filled with the Holy Spirit; you are releasing word curses. When you continuously repeat your negativity against the will and purpose of God in a person's life; you are operating as a witch and warlock. Reader it is so important that we consider our words, to make sure we are not operating in witchcraft. We can not allow satan to use us as instruments of unrighteousness. We must remember our words have power and we can hinder the will of God in the lives of others when we speak against the purposes and plans God has for their lives. We can not allow satan to use us to speak word curses upon others. We must become conscious of what we speak. This is why the Lord wants us to bridle our tongues. Let us examine the scriptures.

PSYCHOLOGICAL WARFARE:
Destroying the Power of Negative Words & Negative Thinking

Proverbs 6: 16-19

These six things doth the LORD hate: yea, seven are an abomination unto him: A proud look, a lying tongue, and hands that shed innocent blood. An heart that deviseth wicked imaginations, feet that be swift in running to mischief, A false witness tear speakers lies, and he that south discord among brethren.

We want to remind you; we will be judge for every secret thing we say and do. With that being said, let us stop allowing satan to use our mouths as a weapon against our loves one. There are so many Christians who will not admit to the secret sin of witchcraft. If you are negative and speaking against people on a daily basis; you are a blind witch and a blind warlock. We recommend you go through the process of inner healing and deliverance and watch your words!

Exodus 22:18

Thou shalt not suffer a witch to live.

PSYCHOLOGICAL WARFARE:
Destroying the Power of Negative Words & Negative Thinking

DESTROYING THE SPIRIT OF WITCHCRAFT

Father in the Name of Jesus Christ, I repent for operating in witchcraft through my words, in Jesus' Name. I admit I have spoken some negative words against Your people, and Your purposes, and Your plans for their lives. Father God, I am asking today for Your forgiveness, in Jesus' Name. Father God, I did not realize that my negative comments, and negative opinions was creating a stumbling block for the other person, in Jesus' Name. I realize my negative words has connected me to the dark kingdom, the kingdom of satan and today I repent, and denounce any involvement in witchcraft through negative evil speaking, in Jesus' Name. I will not operate as a blind witch or a blind wizard, in Jesus' Name. Today I shall destroy the spirit of witchcraft and close every demonic portal that has access to my life through my negative words, and demonic influences, in Jesus' Name. Lord Jesus, I bind all spirits associated with witchcraft, black magic, sorcery, divination, familiar spirits, negative spirits soothsayings, word curses,

PSYCHOLOGICAL WARFARE:
Destroying the Power of Negative Words & Negative Thinking

DESTROYING THE SPIRIT OF WITCHCRAFT
(cont)

chants, voodoo, fortune telling, astro projection, tarot cards, water-witching, crystals, sage, deception, lying casting spells, goddess worship, evil speaking, gossip, evil eye, manipulation, burning demonic candles, necromancy, charms, palm reading, false prophesies, false dreams, pride, psyche readings, psyche prayers, controlling powers, wizardry, witchcraft, incantations, jezebellic spirits and any other unclean practices that I may have done unknown to me, but known by You, Father God, in Jesus' Name. Lord, I ask that You save me, deliver me, and sanctify any gift You have given me, in Jesus' Name. Create in me a clean heart and renew a right spirit within me, in Jesus' Name. I loose the pure spirit of the Holy Ghost, to renew my heart and my mind and to destroy any false beliefs in my life, in Jesus' Name. I bind the spirit of error and I thank You for the Spirit of Truth, and the power of love permeating in my life, in Jesus' Name. Lord, You are my King and the Lord of my life; I ask You to sanctify me wholly and I shall walk in Your divine

PSYCHOLOGICAL WARFARE:
Destroying the Power of Negative Words & Negative Thinking

DESTROYING THE SPIRIT OF WITCHCRAFT
(cont)

will in Jesus' Name. Lord Jesus, I destroy all witchcraft out of my thoughts and my mind. I shall speak truth in my life and the lives of others, in the mighty Name of Jesus Christ, Amen.

PSYCHOLOGICAL WARFARE:
Destroying the Power of Negative Words & Negative Thinking

DEVELOPING A POSITIVE MIND

PSYCHOLOGICAL WARFARE:
Destroying the Power of Negative Words & Negative Thinking

PSYCHOLOGICAL WARFARE:
Destroying the Power of Negative Words & Negative Thinking

Chapter Nine

ADJUSTING YOUR ATTITUDE

After reading the previous chapters, do you see the need for you to change your attitude? **Attitude** deals with your mental state and mental position. It deals with your feelings and emotions concerning a particular issue. Your attitude will determine you altitude. Frankly speaking, your mental disposition can affect your ability to succeed; either positively or negatively. We have all witnessed a person with a hostile state of mind. An attitude of hostility is manifested through aggressive behavior. Some even have an arrogant disposition; people with arrogant attitudes do not listen to others, because they are unteachable and feel they know it all. There are others who can be edgy, snappy, and sharp with their words; they constantly lash out to others with negative comments, ridicule, and sarcasm. These are examples of people who need attitude adjustments. In this

PSYCHOLOGICAL WARFARE:
Destroying the Power of Negative Words & Negative Thinking

chapter, we want to assist you in bringing a mental, emotional, and behavioral balance between your various needs and handling the demands of others. Your mental perception and reactions must change in order to attain a healthy mind. We learned when the mind is bound by the stronghold of negativism; the individual is greatly deceived by the trickery of satan. When he is bombarded by negative thoughts and negative beliefs, his attitude will reveal the power and nature of the strongman that is oppressing the mind. Our mental perceptions, emotions, and behaviors are very much affected by what we hear and perceive within the depth of our souls. Therefore, we must become more discerning about the issues we intake within our ear gates and eye gates. What we see and hear, in our eye gates and ear gates; can increase or decrease our mental abilities. We have to learn how to see and hear God in every situation; because when we understand the purpose of God in life's situations, we can think right thoughts about our lives. The enemy is cunning and a master of deception and often times, he uses people to seed poisonous

PSYCHOLOGICAL WARFARE:
Destroying the Power of Negative Words & Negative Thinking

words in our spirits to change the way we think, perceive, and act. He uses spirits of jealousy, envy, hatred, and fear to bring mental oppression by attacking our thought patterns through negative words. These defiling spirits aim is to detour, distract, and dis-pattern us from achieving our destiny. It is crucial to our mental health to maintain a positive outlook on life, by seeing, hearing, communing, and obeying the Word of God. When we are in proper alignment with God; submitted and thinking the right thoughts, are minds becomes strong and healthy. The power of God is able to destroy mental limitations while healing, and delivering us from unhealthy thoughts and unhealthy emotions. God's power can also shift us into a new paradigm in our thought life, and increase our levels of knowledge and ability to comprehend. This is why it is important for us to judge our mental disposition and go through the process of allowing the Spirit of God to adjust our attitude.

Copyright © DR. CHARISSEE LEWIS, 2017

PSYCHOLOGICAL WARFARE:
Destroying the Power of Negative Words & Negative Thinking

Please complete the exercise below:

Define your daily attitude:_____
_____
_____
_____
_____
_____
_____
_____
_____
_____

Are you optimistic or pessimistic? Explain_____
_____
_____
_____
_____
_____
_____
_____
_____
_____
_____

Copyright © DR. CHARISSEE LEWIS, 2017

PSYCHOLOGICAL WARFARE:
Destroying the Power of Negative Words & Negative Thinking

How do you react when life circumstances does not work in your favor? (Meaning, when you can't have your way.)

_____
_____
_____
_____
_____
_____
_____

How do you cope with anger? (Explain) _____
_____
_____
_____
_____
_____
_____
_____
_____

PSYCHOLOGICAL WARFARE:
Destroying the Power of Negative Words & Negative Thinking

Check what applies to you:

Exposing your attitude when you can not have your way:

__project anger	__get very angry	__fast
__talk about others	__passive anger	__sleep
__reject love ones	__tease others	__escape
__hurt others	__blame others	__pout
__want to run away	__thoughts of leaving	__scream
__tease others	__go to the altar	__swear
__slam doors	__feels guilt	__yell
__smoke a cigarette	__curse someone	__swear
__try to destroy others plans	__become miserable	__fight
__become sullen	__manipulate others	__lie
__drink alcohol	__tease others	__movies
__glutton food	__eat sweets	__hateful
__deceive others	__get jealous	__work
__stop all activity	__insecurity rise	__pills
__pity party	__searching the web	__party
__revengeful	__have sex	__pray
__masturbate	__go to the altar	__porn
__reject self	__self hatred	__rage
__speak negatively	__hear voices	__run
__negative visions	__go shopping	__curse
__smoke weed	__depression	__pray
__withdraw	__read the bible	__mock
__drink liquor/beer	__make others give you money	

Copyright © DR. CHARISSEE LEWIS, 2017

PSYCHOLOGICAL WARFARE:
Destroying the Power of Negative Words & Negative Thinking

Your attitude reveals your thought patterns and affects your behavior. God wants our thoughts to become positive; even when he allows us to see and experience problems. He still wants us to display Christian character.

What is your definition of Christian character?

_____
_____
_____
_____
_____
_____
_____
_____
_____
_____
_____
_____
_____

PSYCHOLOGICAL WARFARE:
Destroying the Power of Negative Words & Negative Thinking

Here are some things you can do to develop your Christian Character:

- Develop a personal relationship with Our Lord & Savior Jesus Christ.
- Repent daily.
- Renew your mind every day by spending time in the presence of the Lord.
- Maintain your strength and work on weaknesses.
- Stay positive in the midst of change.
- Find a positive way to release your anger.
- Practice finding the good in every situation that goes wrong in your life.
- Study Romans 8:28.
- Renew your prayer life.
- Read the word of God daily.
- Become an effective communicator and communicate to others with a heart of love.
- Study the fruits of the Spirit and choose the ones you are weak in and develop them.
- Find new ways of coping when things do not go your way.
- Distance yourself from toxic people, and toxic conversations.
- Do not allow others to seed negative thoughts and negative words into your spirit.

PSYCHOLOGICAL WARFARE:
Destroying the Power of Negative Words & Negative Thinking

PRAYER to ADJUST YOUR ATTITUDE

Father in the Name of Jesus Christ, I come to You humbly with a heart of repentance, seeking Your forgiveness. Father God, forgive me for sins of omission and sins of commission, in Jesus' Name. Father God, I admit my attitude has been moody and negative; I am asking You to forgive me for not representing You with a heart of love, and in the spirit of excellence, in Jesus' Name. Unfortunately, I have been functioning with a negative mindset and a negative disposition. I have been edgy, snappy, sarcastic, and irritated by people who are close to me, and situations occurring in my atmosphere, in Jesus' Name. Lord Jesus, I want to be totally free from all negativity; negative thoughts, negative words, negative emotions, criticism, stress, emotional hurts, emotional stress, damaged emotions, wrong thoughts, distorted thinking, irritation, aggravation, pride, impatience, frustration, mental anguish, judgmental spirits, and controlling spirits, I rebuke theses spirits in Jesus' Name. I veto and cancel every plot of the

Copyright © DR. CHARISSEE LEWIS, 2017

PSYCHOLOGICAL WARFARE:
Destroying the Power of Negative Words & Negative Thinking

PRAYER to ADJUST YOUR ATTITUDE (con't)

enemy which causes my mental disposition to be snappy, snippy, evil, and short-tempered, in Jesus' Name. Lord Jesus, help me to perceive and receive a new outlook on life, and to see myself the way You see me, in Jesus' Name. I denounce low self-esteem, and low self-worth; feelings of inadequacy, and feeling unworthy to be in Your presence, in Jesus' Name. Lord Jesus, I know it is Your love, that causes me to have a healthy mental view of myself, in Jesus' Name. It is Your unconditional agape love, grace, and, mercy which gives me the strength to adjust my attitude. This day I choose to drop the charges against myself, and other people for any wrongs that was done to me, against me, and even by me in Jesus' Name. I am letting go of the past today, and all the baggage and residue of past hurts, in Jesus' Name. I choose to receive love from You; this day I choose to move forward with Your healing virtue, in Jesus' Name. Father God, please show me how to adjust my mind,

PSYCHOLOGICAL WARFARE:
Destroying the Power of Negative Words & Negative Thinking

PRAYER to ADJUST YOUR ATTITUDE (con't)

my attitude, my heart, my thoughts, my emotions, my disposition, and my behavior, in Jesus' Name. Father God, go deep within the corridors of my heart, and pull out every negative seed and every negative weed that is contrary to Your word. Thank You for healing me! My attitude is adjusted in the Mighty Name of Jesus Christ, Amen.

PSYCHOLOGICAL WARFARE:
Destroying the Power of Negative Words & Negative Thinking

Chapter Ten

UNDERSTANDING YOUR VALUE OF YOUR WORDS

There is a spirit world in the universe, which means there is activity taking place in the spiritual world. We must understand whatever we speak will ignite activity in the spirit world. This means if we speak the will of God; the words will come to pass through the authority of God. If we speak negative words; demons are assigned to the negative words to bring them to past. With that being said, the words that we speak are valuable to the destiny of our future. We can not afford to speak words of negativity and death in our lives and in the lives of others. Spiritually speaking, and scientifically speaking, even scientists know there is an action and reaction to everything we say and do. The bible tells us words are spirit and life. The spirit gives life to the words that are spoken. The scripture in the book of John confirms this.......

PSYCHOLOGICAL WARFARE:
Destroying the Power of Negative Words & Negative Thinking

John 6:63

It is the spirit that quickeneth; the flesh profiteth nothing: the words that I speak unto you, they are spirit, and they are life.

Reader, please understand our words are of great worth. We have to become strategic in what we speak. We are a prophetic people with a prophetic purpose to bring to past prophetic fulfillment. Whatever we speak it shall come to past. The bible also tells us death and life are in the power of the tongue, and they that love it shall eat the fruit thereof; in other words, we have what we say. Therefore, we must say the right words. We can shape our lives through what we speak. We can overcome obstacles through what we speak. We can release healing and restoration through the words we speak. We can give confirmation and affirmation through the words we speak. It is time for us to respect the power of our words. In order to do that, we must understand our value of being a Son of God, and the value of what we speak.

Copyright © DR. CHARISSEE LEWIS, 2017

PSYCHOLOGICAL WARFARE:
Destroying the Power of Negative Words & Negative Thinking

As prophetic voices in this earth realm, we have a responsibility to speak words of correction, words of faith, words of kindness, words of wisdom, words of peace, words of righteous, words of healing all in the spirit of love. When we function in the agape love of God, the Holy Spirit changes the sound that comes out of us. We become conscious and convicted when we speak words contrary to the word of God and the Spirit of God. People of God, use your voice as an instrument of righteousness. Bless the people in your atmosphere with the value of your words. You can use your mouth to heal or destroy. Make a conscious decision to speak life into the heart of others, because you are valuable and your words are too!

Exercise: Write down 3 Names you are going to speak life to this entire month.

1) _____

2) _____

3) _____

PSYCHOLOGICAL WARFARE:
Destroying the Power of Negative Words & Negative Thinking

Chapter Eleven

DEVELOPING A HEALTHY SPIRITUAL MIND

The mind is vital to the welfare of man, and a healthy mind is important to have in order to accomplish the ministerial work in the Kingdom of God. Having a healthy mind is not an option; it is a necessity. There are numerous amounts of people, who are oppressed mentality due to unhealthy thoughts and damaged emotions. The mind is comprised of elements in the human body, which causes us to think, will, envision, image, perceive and reason. It is a house for all mental activity. When we look at the behavior of man, our behaviors are determined by what we think in our minds. Every behavior, deed, or action in our lives are first perceived, conceived, and established in the mind of man; and then it is brought forth in the earth. The bible declares, *"For as he thinketh in his heart, so is he:"*,

PSYCHOLOGICAL WARFARE:
Destroying the Power of Negative Words & Negative Thinking

Proverbs 23:7. As human beings, we should always think before we act, and engage in activities. What is phenomenal about the mind is that we cannot think two thoughts simultaneously; we can only think one thought at a time. In other words, according to the scripture above, we are what we think, and the value of our actions is determined by what we choose to think in our minds. Therefore, our thoughts can be true or our thoughts can be false, predicated on who or what we are listening to, in our minds. We should be able to identify the source of our thinking. Is our thought pattern influenced by the Kingdom of God or the Kingdom of Darkness? Is the Holy Spirit speaking in our ears? Or, are demonic spirits speaking in our ears? When we allow wrong thoughts and negative thoughts to enter into our mind; it creates a disposition for unhealthy emotions. Unhealthy emotions are thoughts and feelings which create the wrong mentality. As a result, these unhealthy emotions cause a person to behave and react negatively. When the mind is overwhelmed with negative thoughts and negative emotions it affects our

PSYCHOLOGICAL WARFARE:
Destroying the Power of Negative Words & Negative Thinking

entire being. The enemy constantly tries to high-jack our thoughts; he does this by overloading and bombarding our minds with negative thoughts. On the next few pages, we have listed specifically how negative thinking and negative emotions impact different aspects of our lives. After reading, be opened to identify and confront negative activity in your own life.

THE EFFECTS OF NEGATIVE THINKING & NEGATIVE EMOTIONS

- ❖ **Spiritually** – Negative emotions can affect our spiritual man by attacking our level of faith. If a person is in an environment where words of doubt, fear, anger, jealousy, and rejection are spoken on a consistent basis; it weakens the strength of the spiritual man. The spiritual man is the inner man that communes with God. It has the function of conscience, intuition, and communion. When the spirit of man is constantly hit with negative thoughts and negative emotions, it puts the spiritual man in an oppressive state. It loses its ability of freedom to

PSYCHOLOGICAL WARFARE:
Destroying the Power of Negative Words & Negative Thinking

worship God, and to receive revelation from God. As a result, a person's ability to hear, believe, and obey God is affected in a negative way. The spiritual man must be fed the word of God on a daily basis, so the believer can walk in the spirit and function in the principles of God. The word of God releases an anointing to the spiritual man which is needed to do the work God has called us to do.

Proverbs 18:14: *The spirit of man will sustain his infirmity; but a wounded spirit who can bear?*

Romans 10:17: *So then faith cometh by hearing, and hearing by the word of God.*

❖ **Emotionally** - Negative thinking can damage our emotions and open the door to deadly diseases. When we think the wrong thoughts it can cause stress in our bodies. Emotional stress that is continual and long-term becomes chronic and more destructive to the mind. Negative thinking can produce emotional pain. Emotional pain is suppressed feelings which can cause physical pain. For instance, the pain of a *"heartache"* or *"broken heart"* could be when a person suffers the loss of

PSYCHOLOGICAL WARFARE:
Destroying the Power of Negative Words & Negative Thinking

a love one and does not go through the proper grief process; or, when a spouse experiences the pain of divorce from a marriage. Another example of emotional pain and *"hurt"* is when people falsely accuse us, mock us, reject us, criticize us, and/or judge us. Lastly, emotional pain occurs when a person is not allowed to express their emotions as a child; this could cause them to grow up suppressing, hiding, and devaluing their feeling as adults, which will hinder their ability to receive and express love. When a person is teased, ridiculed, or punished for expressing their emotions, it can affect their self-esteem; causing them to lose their identity by pleasing others regardless of their own feelings. This is a major problem with many people who are experiencing emotional pain, today. As you can see, growing up in a negative environment hearing negative words produces negative emotions. It is my prayer, that you can identify the root of your pain, so you can be healed from the power of negative words, negative thinking, and negative emotions.

PSYCHOLOGICAL WARFARE:
Destroying the Power of Negative Words & Negative Thinking

Luke 4:18: *The Spirit of the Lord is upon me, because he hath anointed me to preach the gospel to the poor; he hath sent me to heal the broken-hearted, to preach deliverance to the captives, and recovering of sight to the blind, to set at liberty them that are bruised,*

Zechariah 3:4: *And he answered and spake unto those that stood before him, saying Take away the filthy garments from him. And caused thine iniquity to pass from thee, and I will clothe thee with change of raiment.*

❖ **Mentally** – Negative words and negative thinking also have a negative effect on the mind. The mind is the house of human thought. It gives us the ability to perceive, create, and think. When the mind is overwhelmed by an atmosphere of negativity, it is attacked by mental anguish and confusion. Mental anguish is great suffering in the mind which is caused by distress, worry, grief, agony, and pain. Confusion is a state of disorder, bewilderment, distraction, embarrassment, and failure to distinguish between difficult things. Negative words and negative thinking open the doors to warfare in the mind. It is important

PSYCHOLOGICAL WARFARE:
Destroying the Power of Negative Words & Negative Thinking

that we identify what comes in our mind, and cast down any defiling thoughts.

Philippians 4:8 *Finally, brethren, whatsoever things are true, whatsoever things are honest, whatsoever things are just, whatsoever things are pure, whatsoever things are lovely, whatever things are of good report; if there be any virtue, and if there be any praise, think on these things.*

II Timothy 1:7 *For God hath not given us the spirit of fear; but of power, and of love, and of a sound mind.*

❖ **Psychologically** – Negative words and negative thinking effects all aspects of the conscious and unconscious mind. They incite the mind to think thoughts of fear, and see visions of fear. Frankly speaking, negative words and negative thinking increase fear in the brain which causes stress to be released in the body. Through study of psychology, we learned that negativity also affects our eating habits, and our sleeping habits. Sometimes, the result of negativity increase emotional eating, and causes sleepless nights. It has been proven negativity disrupt

PSYCHOLOGICAL WARFARE:
Destroying the Power of Negative Words & Negative Thinking

the normal flow of life. So it is imperative for us to protect ourselves from anger, rage, worry, doubt, fear, anxiety, depression and any other negative feelings; all these emotions incite carnal thinking and negative behaviors. The negative words, and negative thoughts interfere with our ability to make sound decisions and to spiritually grow in a healthy manner.

Romans 8:5-6 *For they that are after the flesh do mind the things of the flesh: but they that are after the Spirit. For to be carnally minded is death: but to be spiritually minded is life and peace.*

II Corinthians 4:8 *We are troubled on every side, yet not distressed; we are perplexed, but not in despair; Persecuted, but not forsaken; cast down, but not destroyed;*

❖ **Physically** – The power of negative thoughts and negative words is destructive to every aspect of the human body. Previously, we discussed the affects negativity has on the spirit and the soul of man. Now, let us specifically examine the results of negative thoughts and negative words on the physical body. The

PSYCHOLOGICAL WARFARE:
Destroying the Power of Negative Words & Negative Thinking

power of negativity increases stress and releases toxins in the physical body. Sometimes negative emotions are so strong until they begin to open spiritual doors that gives the enemy access to attack a person in their physical body. There are some diseases that are triggered through toxic emotions due to the connection of the spirit, soul (mind), and body. According to Don Colbert, M. D., we should understand the relationship of the mind-body-spirit; so we can overcome deadly emotions and walk in our physical healing.

PSYCHOLOGICAL WARFARE:
Destroying the Power of Negative Words & Negative Thinking

Don Colbert, M. D. in his book, <u>Deadly Emotions</u> discusses how knowledge of the connection between the spirit, mind, and body could heal or destroy a person. Below, we share some of his discoveries.

1. Anger and Hostility
   ………Hypertension and Coronary Artery Disease

2. Resentment, Bitterness, Self-Hatred, Unforgiveness
   ………Autoimmune Disorders, Rheumatoid Arthritis, Lupus, and Multiple Sclerosis

3. Anxiety
   ……….Irritable Bowel Syndrome, Panic Attacks, Mitral Valve Prolapse, and Heart Palpitations

4. Repressed Anger
   ………Tension and Migrane Headaches, Chronic Back Pain, TMJ, and Fibromyalgia

This are a few of the affects of stress and negativity on the physical body according to Don Colbert, M.D.'s book <u>Deadly Emotions.</u> Reader, it is time to let go of the hurt and pain of negative emotions and be totally free from the

PSYCHOLOGICAL WARFARE:
Destroying the Power of Negative Words & Negative Thinking

thoughts and words of the enemy. Remember, the enemy wants to destroy your spirit, soul (mind), and body. He is calculating in his actions towards humanity. Therefore, we must understand the mental health of a person can have a positive or negative affect on the physical body.

> **Isaiah 53:5** *But he was wounded for our transgressions, He was bruised for our iniquities; The chastisement for our peace was upon Him, and by His stripes we are healed.*

> **III John 2** *Beloved, I wish above all things that thou mayest prosper and be in health, even as thy soul prospereth.*

❖ **Financially** – Negative thoughts and negative words are detrimental to our financial destiny. A person can not prosper successfully with a pessimistic mentality. Our self-talk and belief system must be in alignment with the Word of God. In order to move forward successfully and increase in God economic system for our lives, we need a positive strong mind. The devil works relentlessly to make people feel inadequate when it comes to making money and investing. He wants

PSYCHOLOGICAL WARFARE:
Destroying the Power of Negative Words & Negative Thinking

to delay our determination and crush our faith in God when dealing with our finances. Satan does not want us to accomplish our goals and increase, financially. If he can convince our mind to doubt our abilities; most of the time, people will quit in their mind before they even get started. We must eradicate the deception of negative words and negative thinking. We can not submit to the lies of the enemy. When we are fearful of engaging in the work force; and/or opening and managing our own businesses; we open spiritual doors for the enemy to attack us with poverty, slothfulness, doubt, and procrastination. An impoverished mind is a mind that lacks the strength and vitality to shift into a winning situation. It is a mind that entails thought disturbances. It is also a mind that is poverty-stricken, influenced, and dominated by negativity. We must expose the negative words and negative thoughts and denounce the effects they may have on our abilities to prosper. On the next page, we listed some negative words and phrases the enemy uses to oppress people, financially.

PSYCHOLOGICAL WARFARE:
Destroying the Power of Negative Words & Negative Thinking

NEGATIVE WORDS and BEHAVIORS THAT AFFECT WEALTH POTENTIAL

poor	inadequate	unqualified	convict
weak	tired	old	scared
fearful	dumb	penniless	never
can't	drained	debt	lack
doubt	skepticism	unbelief	selfish
insecurities	envy	no	more
shortage	want	need	closed
jealousy	lazy	trifling	lazy
oppression	greed	unrealistic	broke
depressed	death	defeated	divorce
insufficiency	late	homeless	stress
limitations	error	confusion	owe
distractions	exhausted	broken	tired
destructive	wasteful	eviction	hurt
burdens	embezzlement	waste	hungry
negative	procrastination	stealing	death
religious	attitude	deception	evil
excessive	manipulation	scams	schemes
borrow	problems	underpaid	loss
heaviness	workaholic	disorganization	user

Copyright © DR. CHARISSEE LEWIS, 2017

PSYCHOLOGICAL WARFARE:
Destroying the Power of Negative Words & Negative Thinking

NEGATIVE THOUGHTS THAT AFFECTS OUR WEALTH POTENTIAL

1) I will never get out of debt.
2) Will I never my finances ever change?
3) We don't ever have enough.
4) Money comes, money go.
5) We just don't have enough.
6) I'm just tired of working.
7) I'm not giving nothing to the church.
8) Every time I turn around somebody is asking for money.
9) I'm about to max out this credit card.
10) I'm broke.
11) Don't ask me for nothing.
12) I'm tired of folks begging for my money.
13) I'm going to shop til I drop.
14) I'm spending everything.
15) I'll go broke before I give her anything
16) I don't want to work.
17) I can't do that; it's for rich folks.
18) I want it, and I will take theirs.
19) You're going to give me that money.
20) Only rich people can invest.

Copyright © DR. CHARISSEE LEWIS, 2017

PSYCHOLOGICAL WARFARE:
Destroying the Power of Negative Words & Negative Thinking

It is our prayer, that you denounce the negative words and negative thoughts and phrases we shared on the previous pages.

A HEALTHY SPIRITUAL MIND

In the other chapters, we discussed the challenges we are confronted with, when bound by the stronghold of negativism. We shared with you, how negative words and negative thoughts place believers in a dimension of psychological warfare. However in this chapter, we shared the affects of negativity spiritually, emotionally, mentally, physically, psychologically, and financially. Our aim is to gradually unfold the benefits of expanding and increasing our mental capabilities from the negative to the positive; from being a carnal-minded person to becoming a spiritual-minded person. I am speaking of a paradigm shift; to shift from carnality to spirituality.

PSYCHOLOGICAL WARFARE:
Destroying the Power of Negative Words & Negative Thinking

To begin with, in order to change our mind from the carnal to the spiritual; we must first accept the love of Jesus Christ in all the unregenerate areas in our lives. The unregenerate areas are the issues of darkness, where satan still holds us captive. These are areas in our mind which causes us to behave, react, and respond to the mannerism of the old man. They are also issues that are hidden in the corridor of our minds. They are issues of unconfessed sin, which separate us from God. When we allow the light of God's word to shine on these dark areas, we are able to expose the deception of satan and repent of our sins. This is very important to the development of the mind; because we have to trust God to deliver us from the fears of satanic spirits whose assignment is to keep us bound to our past. Our Father God wants us to develop the mind of Christ. This is the kind of mind that connects us to our Father God. This is a mind of humility. A mind of humility understands the importance of love and the value of servitude causing us to be willing to do the work of the Kingdom, without being judgmental.

PSYCHOLOGICAL WARFARE:
Destroying the Power of Negative Words & Negative Thinking

Philippians 2:4-5

Look not to every man on his things, but every man also on the things of others.
Let this mind be in you, which was also in Christ Jesus.

I Peter 4:1

Forasmuch then as Christ hath suffered for us in the flesh, arm yourselves likewise with the same mind: for he that hath suffered in the flesh hath ceased from sin, That he no longer should live the rest of his time in the flesh to the lusts of men, but to the will of God.

The Lord wants us to come out of pride and to put away our lustful thinking. The only way this can be accomplished is through the word of God. The scripture tells us that we must suffer in the flesh. We have to learn how to deny our flesh from the lusts that it desires. This process has already taken place if you walked through the spiritual exercises we comprised in the previous chapters. Satan wants us to keep a carnal mind so he can continue to use, and abuse us. The bible tells to be carnally minded is death, but to be spiritually minded is life and peace, according to **Romans 8:5.**

Copyright © DR. CHARISSEE LEWIS, 2017

PSYCHOLOGICAL WARFARE:
Destroying the Power of Negative Words & Negative Thinking

In conclusion, it is time for us to start pleasing God. We can no longer process our thoughts through carnal negative thinking. We must change our thought patterns from the carnal to the spiritual. A spiritual mind is a mind that is operating through the foundation of the word of God. A spiritual mind is a mind that is God-conscious. It is a mind that is balanced in its attitude, thoughts, character, and behavior. Now that you have experienced the process of inner healing and deliverance: it is time to engage in a curriculum of transformation and development for a healthy spiritual mind.

PSYCHOLOGICAL WARFARE:
Destroying the Power of Negative Words & Negative Thinking

Please read the following passage and answer the questions below: *Romans 8:5-10*

1. What are some of the fleshly things you do that are not pleasing to God?

_____
_____
_____
_____
_____
_____

2. In the reading, what does it mean to mind the things of the flesh?

_____
_____
_____
_____
_____
_____

3. What does it mean to mind the things of the spirit?

_____
_____
_____
_____
_____
_____

Copyright © DR. CHARISSEE LEWIS, 2017

PSYCHOLOGICAL WARFARE:
Destroying the Power of Negative Words & Negative Thinking

4. What is the nature of a spiritual mind?

_____
_____
_____
_____
_____
_____
_____
_____

5. What is the nature of a carnal mind?

_____
_____
_____
_____
_____
_____
_____
_____

6. Identify and write down the things in your life that are hindering you from maintaining a spiritual mind.

_____
_____
_____
_____
_____
_____
_____
_____

PSYCHOLOGICAL WARFARE:
Destroying the Power of Negative Words & Negative Thinking

7. Write down un-confessed sin in your life.

_____
_____
_____
_____
_____
_____

8. Name five spiritual activities you engaged in, which changed your life.

_____
_____
_____
_____
_____
_____

9. What do you think are the results of living in the spirit?

_____
_____
_____
_____
_____
_____

PSYCHOLOGICAL WARFARE:
Destroying the Power of Negative Words & Negative Thinking

PRAYER to DEVELOP a HEALTHY SPIRITUAL MIND

Father in the Name of Jesus Christ, Lord I repent today for all un-confessed sin, _____ (name the issues of sin). Lord, I realize I have been hiding behind the spirit of pride. There are issues, thoughts, and ideals in my mind that are contrary to Your word. Today, I chose to humble myself before Your throne, in Jesus' Name. I ask for Your forgiveness for not submitting and yielding sooner, in Jesus' Name. I no longer want to walk in darkness in this area of my life, but I am exposing the tricks and lies of Satan on today. I believe in the power of the Holy Spirit and I receive Your love, in Jesus' Name. Lord Jesus Christ, You are the head of my life and I submit myself before Your throne. I desire a healthy spiritual mind with healthy thoughts and healthy emotions, in Jesus' Name. Lord, I need a paradigm shift in my mind, in Jesus' Name. Lord, heal my mind, my will, my emotions, my imagination, my memory, and my intellect, in Jesus' Name. I desire to change the way

Copyright © DR. CHARISSEE LEWIS, 2017

PSYCHOLOGICAL WARFARE:
Destroying the Power of Negative Words & Negative Thinking

PRAYER to DEVELOP a HEALTHY SPIRITUAL MIND (con't)

I think, perceive, react, and respond, in Jesus' Name. I rebuke all demonic thoughts, and negative emotions. I shall change my practices beginning today and cover my mind with the blood of Jesus Christ and meditate on Your scriptures this day I am a new creature in You. Thank You, Father God for Your unconditional love, in Jesus' Name, Amen!

Believers, it is so crucial that we think the right thoughts, and speak the right words. The enemy's aim is to use the spirit of deception to try to infiltrate the mind to alter the thought life of the believer. He is a master at deception, and when he deceives the mind into thinking wrong; the words and behavior of a person will manifest through negative actions. It is imperative for us to continuously develop a healthy spiritual mind by participating in some mental exercises. These mental exercises can assist us in understanding God and renewing our mind to receive

PSYCHOLOGICAL WARFARE:
Destroying the Power of Negative Words & Negative Thinking

the word of God. They also make us spiritually mature giving us mental strength and stability to identify and confront old patterns of thinking. We share some examples below.

MENTAL EXERCISES TO BUILD A HEALTHY MIND:

1) **Practice Developing Patterns of Positive Thinking:** Practice thinking positive thoughts. Be conscious of what you are thinking and do not allow negative thoughts to enter your mind. Build you thoughts from what the Holy Spirit is speaking to you. Build your thoughts from the Word of God, because whatever we think affect our emotions.

2) **Practice the Pattern of Memorization:** Practice memorizing the scriptures. When we read the Scriptures we can commit the scriptures to our conscience and sub-conscience to store, retain, and remember. The Holy Spirit will bring up the scriptures we store, when we need them.

PSYCHOLOGICAL WARFARE:
Destroying the Power of Negative Words & Negative Thinking

MENTAL EXERCISES TO BUILD A HEALTHY MIND: (con't)

3) **Practice the Pattern of Learning New Knowledge, New Words, New Information, and New Revelation:** Practice being receptive to the newness of life and the newness of Christ. We have the ability to replace, confront, and crush the old thought paradigms by receiving the new.

4) **Practice the Pattern of Meditation:** Practice meditating on the word of God. The bible tells us to meditate day and night. Christian meditation entails extracting truth out of the Logos word of God until it becomes a Rhema word. This requires us to focus our minds quietly on what the Holy Spirit is saying and to understand and receive revelation knowledge.

5) **Practice the Pattern of Visualization:** Practice Visualization means to allow the Holy Spirit access to communicate with our inner man

PSYCHOLOGICAL WARFARE:
Destroying the Power of Negative Words & Negative Thinking

MENTAL EXERCISES TO BUILD A HEALTHY MIND: (con't)

(spiritual man) the messages from God into our minds through visual revelation. The Father will show us what He wants us to see through the power of visualizing. It is all inspire by Him.

6) **Practice Maintaining a Positive Attitude:** Practice developing a positive outlook on life. Engage in activities that help you to feel good about you. your attitude is a disposition of your mind. When you are happy about your life; you are mentally positioned to be happy for others.

7) **Practice Guarding Your Eyes and Ears:** Practice guarding what you see and hear. We have a responsibility to cover our spiritual and natural eyes and ears. The enemy constantly looks for ways to seed corruption and perversion in our spirit, soul, and body. We must be strategic and discerning to protects ourselves from satan.

PSYCHOLOGICAL WARFARE:
Destroying the Power of Negative Words & Negative Thinking

You are on your way to developing a healthy spiritual mind, speak the word, read the word, live in the word, saturate your spirit and mind with the word of God. Reader, do not allow satan to take you back to that old negative thinking. Remember, satan is the master of deception and a murderer. The Bible, says he is the father of lies and there is no truth in him, according to the book of St. John,

John 8:44

Ye are of *your* father the devil, and the lusts of your father ye will do. He was a murderer from the beginning and abode not in the truth, because there is no truth in him. When he speaketh a lie, he speaketh of his own: for he is a liar, and the father of it.

John 10:10

The thief cometh not, but for to steal, and to kill, and to destroy: I am come that they might have life, and that they might have is more abundantly.

Walk in the newness of Jesus Christ and you shall live a life of peace and fulfillment, this is one of the promises of God when we develop the mind of Christ!

PSYCHOLOGICAL WARFARE:
Destroying the Power of Negative Words & Negative Thinking

Chapter Twelve

A Beautiful Positive Mind

The Beauty of a positive mind bears a heavenly sound that attracts the attention of heaven and an indescribable sweetness and strength; that confounds the agents of satan. The beauty of a positive mind bears characteristics in an individual that connects with the love of God and the power of God. The positive mind is able to see the best in others, regardless of their sins or imperfections. This kind of mind is beautiful, because it is able to love unconditionally. It operates in the agape love of God. It understands the battles of life. It has experienced the rejection of man, depths of pain, the persecution of words, the bruising of heartaches and heartbreaks; and yet, it has gone through the process of inner healing and deliverance. The beautiful positive mind is a mind that has been renewed by the word of God. It is a mind that is influenced by the Holy Spirit. It is

PSYCHOLOGICAL WARFARE:
Destroying the Power of Negative Words & Negative Thinking

a regenerated mind. A mind filled with divine thoughts; the thoughts of God. This kind of mind is strong, because it is receptive to God's thoughts. The beautiful positive mind has the mind of Christ. The mind of Christ is a mind ready and willing to do the work of the Kingdom. It is mind whose aim is to please Our Father God. It understands there is a higher call and purpose to be accomplished. This kind of mind is clear, pure, and positive. It is free from the pollution of negativity. It can easily identify the thoughts of the devil. The beautiful positive mind is God-conscious, motivated by the principles, and precepts of the word of God. It is able to communicate with our Lord & Savior Jesus Christ. It is a spiritual mind. It has access to heavenly realms and new dimensions in the Kingdom of God. It is a mind of purpose and vision, with capabilities of seeing afar off. This mind is able to strategize and invade and shut down demonic systems through prayer and intercession. A beautiful positive mind is a mind that is trustworthy and God shares His secrets with the likes of this kind of mind. This mind is adventurous

PSYCHOLOGICAL WARFARE:
Destroying the Power of Negative Words & Negative Thinking

and sees no failure in new assignments. This is a courageous and triumphant mind. This mind is humble, and yet bold. This mind is simple and yet superb in the work of God. This mind function in the anointing and the authority of God. This beautiful positive mind is your New Mind.

Reader, throughout this book we made it simple for you to identify areas of negativity in your mind. It is our prayer that you have engaged fully in the assignments and exercises we provided for the healing and deliverance of your mind. We know satan is a destroyer and he wants to stop the positivity, peace, progression, and prosperity in your life. This is why we laid great emphasis on the exercises for identification of inner healing and deliverance. If you truly read the book in its entirety, and engaged yourself in the exercises; you are in the midst of a paradigm shift and you will conquer all the negative words and negative thoughts that has been interfering with your mental abilities! You are destined for a great future with a great mind! God is

PSYCHOLOGICAL WARFARE:
Destroying the Power of Negative Words & Negative Thinking

working in obscurity on your behalf! Be healed in your mind, stay free of negativity in word and deed! Walk in your purpose with a beautiful positive mind!

PSYCHOLOGICAL WARFARE:
Destroying the Power of Negative Words & Negative Thinking

PRAYER OF SALVATION

Father God, in the Name of Jesus Christ, Lord I ask You to forgive me for all my sins: sins of omission and sins of commission. Today, I denounce satan out of my life. I repent of any association with the spirit of Lucifer, confusion, and chaotic spirits. Lord, I want to be saved, sanctified, delivered, and purified from the influence, oppression, depression, suppression, and regression of satan. I bind ancient strongholds out of my mind. Lord, I choose You, Jesus Christ, to be the Lord over my life, as my personal Savior. I believe You died on the cross for my sins, so I can have a right to eternal life. I believe in the blood atonement of the cross. I believe You are Lord over the entire universe. I believe You can heal and deliver me from all of my troubles. I believe in the power of the Holy Ghost. Your word declares, if I confess with my mouth and believe in my heart that God hath raised Jesus Christ from the dead, I shalt be saved, according to Romans 10:9, in the Name of Jesus Christ, Amen!

PSYCHOLOGICAL WARFARE:
Destroying the Power of Negative Words & Negative Thinking

Dr. Charissee is available for prophetic counseling, prayer, seminars, speaking engagements, conferences and retreats.

For appointments, booking engagements or tape listings contact:

LIQUID FIRE TRAINING CENTER
1911 Horger St.
Lincoln Park, Michigan 48146
Phone: (313) 544-8010

WEBSITE: WWW. DRCHARISSEELEWIS.COM
Email: Drcharisseelewis@icloud.com

Other books available:

A Basic Guide to Spiritual Warfare

Building a Strong Prayer Wall

Destroying the Spirit of Witchcraft

Dream Journal: Understanding Dream Language & Interpretation

Dreams & Visions: The Ministry of the Seer

It's My Time Now! Prayer Journal

It's Time to Soar

Liquid Fire School of the Prophetic: Basic

Liquid Fire School of the Prophetic: Intermediate

Love on Fire

Moving From Pain to Power

Paganism: The Truth about Christmas

PSYCHOLOGICAL WARFARE:
Destroying the Power of Negative Words & Negative Thinking

Prophetic Warfare

Revived & Winning on Every Side

Releasing the Voice of Prophetic Order

Satanism: The Truth about Halloween

Searching for God through Intimacy

Surviving Wounds of the Heart

Surviving Wounds of the Heart Workbook

The Joy & Pain of a Mother & Daughter Relationship

The Joy & Pain of a Mother & Daughter Relationship Workbook

The Trying times of an Anointed Woman of God
The Truth about Halloween
Who's Fighting for the Children?
Worship Live at the Altar

PSYCHOLOGICAL WARFARE:
Destroying the Power of Negative Words & Negative Thinking

www.ingramcontent.com/pod-product-compliance
Lightning Source LLC
Chambersburg PA
CBHW081152290426
44108CB00018B/2527